The Advisory Committee Advantage:
Creating an Effective Strategy for Programmatic Improvement

by Lee Teitel

ASHE-ERIC Higher Education Report No. 1, 1994

Prepared by

Clearinghouse on Higher Education
The George Washington University

In cooperation with

Association for the Study
of Higher Education

Published by

School of Education and Human Development
The George Washington University

Jonathan D. Fife, Series Editor

Cite as
Teitel, Lee 1994. *The Advisory Committee Advantage: Creating an Effective Strategy for Programmatic Improvement.* ASHE-ERIC Higher Education Report No. 1. Washington, D.C.: The George Washington University, School of Education and Human Development.

Library of Congress Catalog Card Number 94-73327
ISSN 0884-0040
ISBN 1-878380-57-5

Managing Editor: Bryan Hollister
Manuscript Editor: Barbara Fishel, Editech
Cover design by Michael David Brown, Rockville, Maryland

The ERIC Clearinghouse on Higher Education invites individuals to submit proposals for writing monographs for the *ASHE-ERIC Higher Education Report* series. Proposals must include:
1. A detailed manuscript proposal of not more than five pages.
2. A chapter-by-chapter outline.
3. A 75-word summary to be used by several review committees for the initial screening and rating of each proposal.
4. A vita and a writing sample.

ERIC **Clearinghouse on Higher Education**
School of Education and Human Development
The George Washington University
One Dupont Circle, Suite 630
Washington, DC 20036-1183

This publication was prepared partially with funding from the Office of Educational Research and Improvement, U.S. Department of Education, under contract no. ED RR-93-0200. The opinions expressed in this report do not necessarily reflect the positions or policies of OERI or the Department.

EXECUTIVE SUMMARY

Advisory committees are effective ways to help connect universities and colleges to their environments. Interest in advisory committees has increased in recent years as institutions of higher education and their programs face intense challenges in adapting to and meeting today's needs. Driven, in many cases, by declining enrollments and/or diminishing budgets, institutions find themselves under increased pressure to do more with less. At the same time, demands and expectations for responsiveness and accountability have increased, requiring greater interaction with the world outside the ivory tower. Advisory committees represent a "bridge to the external public" (Thompson 1984, p. 27), and the growth of interest in advisory committees shares its roots with the recent surge of attention to strategic planning and total quality management. Advisory committees can provide mechanisms at all levels of higher education to help improve communication and interaction with the outside world. They can provide fresh insights, powerful connections, access to valuable resources, and excellent public relations. In conjunction with a strategic plan or total quality management, they can be key elements in renewing and revitalizing an institution.

What Are Advisory Committees? What Do They Do?

The simple definition of an advisory committee is *a group of volunteers that meets regularly on a long-term basis to provide advice and/or support to an institution or one of its subunits.* Advisory committees can range from those that consult to university presidents on the broadest of policy issues (Scott 1988) to committees that focus on the nitty-gritty—what machine shop tools a community college should buy, for example (Corley 1988). By opening a window of exchange with members of the broader society, advisory committees can help institutions with a host of important functions: strengthening programs, improving management, reviewing and evaluating mission, programs, and services, recruiting personnel, raising funds, promoting public relations, and improving relationships with other organizations (Cuninggim 1985, pp. 5–16). The first three functions, and sometimes the fourth, are truly advisory in nature, as the committee provides external input into internal processes; the last three fall more into the support category, with committee members serving the organization by helping *in* the outside world.

What Is an Effective Advisory Committee?

The level of the advisory committee's work varies tremendously along a spectrum of involvement and activity. Some committees exist in name only and have never met or, after one organizational meeting, go on for years on paper. Others meet once or twice annually, for largely ceremonial purposes. Others are largely a collection of advisers who might individually provide advice or support but whose committees rarely, if ever, meet. At the other end of the spectrum are occasionally overinvolved advisory committees. They provide advice where none is wanted, and they get involved in affairs that should be left for program directors, staff, or faculty.

Effective advisory committees avoid both extremes. They are committees that meet regularly and work together to provide advice and/or support that contributes significantly to the program's or institution's improvement. Even within this definition of effectiveness, however, can be a broad range of activity. Some advisory committees serve mostly as boosters, raising funds, providing connections to outside resources, promoting public relations, and, in general, providing important support and service while offering little or no advice. Although not technically "advisory," they are included here because they are a common type of advisory committee and because they can make significant contributions to a program. Committees that do provide advice range from those whose focus and direction are carefully directed by the staff, administration, or faculty to those with significant independence whose advice covers a wide scope and range of topics. Some committees provide service as well as advice.

How Many Advisory Committees Are Effective?

Determining how many advisory committees are effective is difficult for two reasons. First, not everyone agrees on the definition of effectiveness. Some deans or program directors, for instance, might be happy with a ceremonial committee comprised of high-profile individuals in the community who meet once a year and say nice things about the program. Other administrators, who reluctantly establish an advisory group because of an external mandate, might be pleased to have it exist solely on paper. Some deans might be very happy to have a committee of advisers to call on for individual consultation and advice. Such committees do not meet the earlier definition of an effective advisory committee, however, because they do not work together to contribute significantly to the program's or institution's improvement.

Second, studies of advisory committees' effectiveness are very rare. Institutions might list their advisory committees in their bulletins and reports, but they are unlikely to collect information about their effectiveness and even less likely to report it in the literature. The few existing studies on effectiveness are in the vocational education and community college sectors and were conducted by outside agencies that contacted committee members directly. They document the widespread existence of paper committees whose "members" did not even know they were "serving" (Massachusetts Dept. of Education 1985, 1986). Other, anecdotal evidence also suggests that many programs and institutions do not effectively use their advisory committees for advice or support (Axelrod 1991; Laney 1984).

What Makes an Advisory Committee Effective?

An advisory group is more likely to be effective at providing advice and support when:

1. Institutional representatives (deans, directors, staff, faculty) genuinely desire the committee's input;
2. The committee is comprised of knowledgeable, committed individuals whose interest in volunteering their own time is sustained by appropriate recognition and rewards;
3. The committee's group processes and procedures for governance allow for regular meetings, a sense of engagement and ownership, and sufficient access to information about the program or institution so that the committee can offer useful advice and support;
4. The expectations about the roles of the committee in providing advice and support are clear, consistent, and well communicated.

How Can Those Working with Advisory Committees Improve Their Effectiveness?

The staff, faculty, and administrators who work with advisory committees need to think through how much support and/or advice they really want. Advisory groups, although they afford great potential, usually require additional work for management and can complicate matters. Institutional representatives need to decide what kinds of support or how much advice they want and then clearly communicate it to potential committee members. The greatest source of dissatisfaction with advisory committees comes from poor communications and a mismatch of expectations. Potential members who accept an invitation to join an advisory committee to provide advice and input are usually pleased and even proud to be recognized for their "acknowledged expertise" (Light 1982), but if they find themselves in a ceremonial role, lacking the information and the opportunity to make a contribution to the program, they can become quite disgruntled. Many such problems can be avoided if institutional representatives clearly and consistently communicate their expectations for the committee's roles in advice and service. Similarly, individuals invited to serve on an advisory committee should seek information about expectations and roles before they say "yes."

The potential benefits of advisory committees in a program's improvement are enormous, but for many advisory committees, the potential is not fully realized.

CONTENTS

FOREWORD

Throughout the history of higher education in the United States, boards and committees with some members from outside the organization have been used to help guide an institution's internal activities. The purpose of these advisory committees was to ensure that the institution kept to its mission—which was often defined by the board. Similarly, many doctoral dissertation committees contained members from outside the academic program to provide greater expertise and peer review.

This tradition of seeking advice from outside the academy is taking on a more important role as academic leaders realize that, properly used, advisory committees can be very useful in directing, supporting, and furthering the organization's goals. When the membership of a committee includes representatives of the beneficiaries of the organization's services, it can be very useful in offering advice to make those services even more effective. For an academic program educating students for a specific career, an advisory committee's membership could include students and employers whose primary responsibility is to offer advice on the skills and knowledge needed for success in a career. For a center on policy studies, an advisory committee could generate discussion on the most significant or promising areas for policy research. And for administrative areas, such as buildings and grounds, an advisory committee could help the institution stay up to date on the latest products and equipment that would help to keep maintenance costs as low as possible.

The potential of advisory committees to be a positive force for any organization depends upon its leadership. First, that leadership must believe that it will be able to work more satisfactorily if it seeks advice and guidance from people who have an interest in the success of their organization. The leaders must realize that useful advisory committees do not just happen: Meetings must be carefully planned and followed through consistently. The committee's membership must be selected in consideration of the committee's mission and desired outcomes, and membership should not be offered without a clear understanding about expectations.

Sometimes, committees can be very useful; sometimes, they are not. One rule of good management for administrators is never to ask for advice that they plan not to take, for when advice is sought but not used, the organization loses credibility. Eventually, it will affect the organization's ability to maintain external support.

On the whole, institutions of higher education have underused the advantages that advisory committees can provide for several reasons: the belief that outsiders cannot contribute to the goals of the institution or its subunits; the fear that advisory committees will get involved in areas where they do not belong; and the uncertainties created by stories of advisory committees that were disruptive and at times destructive.

The biggest reason that advisory committees have not been used or have been underused, however, is a lack of understanding about how to use and manage them. This report on developing effective advisory committees by Lee Teitel, assistant professor of educational administration at the University of Massachusetts at Boston, reviews the use and management of advisory committees. It examines the purpose and advantages of an advisory committee, discusses the determinants of an effective committee, and recommends ways to start and sustain an effective advisory committee.

Knowing how to get the most from advisory committees can help organizations succeed in ways they could not imagine. It is a low-cost way to bring normally high-priced individuals together to work collectively on very specific issues. Depending on the purpose of the committee, the results can vary from just better visibility to developing a plan of action that can result in millions of dollars of new support. The first step is knowing how and when to use advisory committees. This report will contribute greatly to starting the process on a firm foundation.

Jonathan D. Fife
Series Editor, Professor and
Director, ERIC Clearinghouse on Higher Education

ACKNOWLEDGMENTS

Thanks to Dan Seymour, who got me started on this project, to the anonymous reviewers who helped me finish it, and to my family and Fourth Lake friends who helped keep me going along the way. My appreciation also to the individuals who were interviewed for this report and whose contributions were vital in helping me understand the important issues about advisory committees.

A special thanks to Laura Derman, my wife and life-long partner, for her suggestions, her wisdom, and her clear thinking, as well as her love and support. This book is dedicated to her and to our three children, Joanna, Becky, and Emma.

INTRODUCTION

*Whether or not you have an advisory group is strictly
optional (unless dictated by your funding source). Your
decision should reflect your personal style and the way you
perceive your purposes and needs. Some programs find
advisory boards unnecessary. Others find them an outright
pain in the neck to be avoided at all cost. . . . [And] still
others find advisory boards a decided asset and rely heavily
upon [members'] skills, contacts, and . . . opinions . . .*
(Borden 1984, pp. II-1, II-2).

What determines whether an advisory committee will be
unnecessary, a pain in the neck, or a decided asset to an institution or program? What motivates people to serve on advisory committees? How much advice do program directors,
deans, and faculty who work with advisory committees really
want? If staff and committee members have differences of
opinion about the proper role of the committee, how should
they be resolved? Why do some advisory committees make
active and vibrant contributions to their organizations for years
and years, while others never meet or serve solely as rubber
stamps? What practices and procedures foster the most effective advisory groups? And what exactly is an effective advisory
committee?

*What exactly
is an effective
advisory
committee?*

These questions and others frame this Higher Education
Report. It is designed to provide a practical guide to effective
institutional and programmatic advisory committees for colleges, universities, and nonprofit organizations. It should be
of interest to chancellors, presidents, provosts, deans, department heads, program directors, faculty and staff members,
and executive directors of nonprofit organizations who have
occasion to work with advisory committees. It will also be
of interest to committee members and policy makers concerned about how public funds are spent or to other outsiders
interested in the way institutions of higher education and nonprofit organizations respond to and meet society's needs.

The report is comprised of three parts. The first, including
the first three sections, defines advisory committees and why
they are established; explores why an institution or program
might set up an advisory committee; identifies how advisory
committees help connect organizations to their environments
and how they dovetail with institutional efforts at improvement like strategic planning or total quality management; and
examines the growing external pressures to mandate advisory

committees in some settings. The first part concludes with a historical case study of what happens when funding sources mandate advisory committees. It summarizes the history of the sector of education with the longest involvement with mandated advisory committees—vocational education—and illustrates the growing use of mandated advisory committees and the expansion of their roles, the history of their perceived ineffectiveness, and strategies that have been used to overcome this ineffectiveness.

The second part, including the next four sections, examines the factors that determine an advisory committee's effectiveness, noting that effective advisory committees have found the balance between underinvolvement and overinvolvement. It explores three broad factors contributing to effective committees: the attitudes and expectations of staff and administrators, the motivations and commitments of the committee members, and the group dynamics that take place when they function as a committee. The part also concludes with a case study—about a mandated advisory committee that tried to establish its independence.

The final part, comprised of the last two sections, includes recommendations for more effective advisory committees. It summarizes the practical advice of dozens of articles and books on how to set up an advisory committee and run meetings. It also, however, acknowledges that not all staff, directors, or deans always want a highly active committee and suggests ways to try to get the kind of advisory committee they want. It advises committee members and potential members about how their hopes and expectations can be met through involvement with an advisory committee and explores the implications of this more relativistic (but possibly more realistic) approach to advisory committees.

WHAT ARE ADVISORY COMMITTEES?

The Simple Definition

Simply defined, an advisory committee is *a group of volunteers that meets regularly on a long-term basis to provide advice and/or support to an institution or one of its subunits.* Names, however, are frequently used imprecisely: "Visiting" and "advisory," "committees," "councils," and "boards" are often used interchangeably, making a confusing array of possible names for such committees. Worse, names are sometimes used inconsistently, and one college's visiting committee is strictly advisory, while another's is a governing body (Cuninggim 1985). Consequently, it is worthwhile to look closely at the defining characteristics of advisory committees to help sort through the maze of committees, councils, boards, and commissions that proliferates in higher education.

> • *An advisory committee is a group of volunteers . . .*

This first, and most basic, distinction separates advisory committees from internal committees comprised of faculty, paid staff, or administrators. Implicit in the definition of an advisory committee is that it is made up largely, if not entirely, of people from outside the organization. When properly configured, an advisory committee should provide a "bridge to the external public" (Thompson 1984, p. 27). Although this ideal is implicit, it is not always reached, occasionally prompting controversy over the committee's membership. For example, a study of the 106 citizen advisory committees on services for handicapped students that California community colleges had to establish shows that college faculty and staff made up the largest group of advisory committee members (Baker and Ostertag 1981). The report recommends that composition of the committees be changed to better reflect community members. Similarly, a review of advisory committees in allied health programs notes that, despite the state-issued guidebooks' prohibiting faculty from being voting members (to ensure that the advisory committee "does not act simply [as] a rubber stamp for the program"), all of the programs allowed it; one even *limited* membership to faculty (Gross 1980, p. 25). Frequently, mandated advisory committees specify percentages of certain populations to constitute the committee as a way of ensuring that advisory committees bring outside input into the institution.

Occasionally, universities set up "advisory committees" comprised of faculty or staff "volunteers" from other subunits, but such an arrangement is usually called an *"internal* advisory committee." For example, universitywide advisory committees can be a critical means of legitimatizing and gaining support for nontraditional programs in a large university (Welch 1989). Internal advisory groups help build bridges between sectors of a large institution.

• . . . *that meets regularly on a long-term basis* . . .

This phrase distinguishes advisory committees from other groups that might have a specific short-term charge, such as blue ribbon commissions or specialized task forces. Like advisory committees, blue ribbon commissions use outside expertise to address educational issues, but they differ in that they are of fixed duration, have authority given by a legislature or executive branch, have their own staff and funding, and usually have a regional or statewide focus (Johnson 1982). Advisory groups differ from other committees at an institution that are focused on particular tasks, such as search committees (Bromert 1984), or ad hoc advisory groups set up for a particular and short-lived purpose, such as planning before a particular activity or dealing with a specific problem that arises in the course of a program (Thompson 1984). "Long-term" also distinguishes an advisory committee from visiting committees or teams that come to an institution for a day or two as part of accreditation or program review. Such short-lived teams would investigate some aspect(s) of the institution, write a report, and disband (Laney 1984).

• . . . *to provide advice and/or support* . . .

Advisory committees differ from boards of regents, trustees, or governing boards because they lack fiduciary or legal authority for the organization or program. Several essential differences can be found:

The function of governing boards is to control and assist. They have the ultimate decision-making authority, responsibility, and liability for all aspects of the organization. The function of advisory boards, on the other hand, is to provide assistance, to advise, and to make recommendations. Unlike governing boards, they have no power to make policy deci-

sions, nor are they legally responsible for managing and supervising the organization (Caparosa 1984, p. 44).

The work of advisory committees falls into two main categories: *advising* the institution by bringing outside perspectives into internal processes, and *supporting* the college or university by operating in the external environment in ways that benefit it.

Of the seven functions of an advisory committee shown in table 1, the first three—strengthening the program(s), improving the institution's management, reviewing and evaluating the institution's mission, programs, and services—and sometimes the fourth—recruiting personnel—are primarily advisory in nature. Each task involves use of outside expertise so its influence will be internally felt. In performing these roles, the advisory committee provides a conduit for people outside the organization to help shape it and perhaps have an influence on decision making.

TABLE 1

FUNCTIONS OF ADVISORY COMMITTEES

- To strengthen the program(s)
- To improve the institution's management
- To review and evaluate the institution's mission, programs, and services
- To recruit personnel
- To raise funds
- To promote public relations
- To improve the institution's relationships with other organizations

Source: Cuninggim 1985, pp. 5–16.

The last three roles—raising funds, promoting public relations, and improving the institution's relationships with other organizations—while also providing input (in the form of money, for instance), are qualitatively different. Advisory committees performing these roles provide support or service. Unlike the first three items on the list, the sphere of influence and operation is external; that is, advisory committee members reach out into the community to raise money, promote public relations, or facilitate relationships with others.

Advisory committees can be set up to offer advice on virtually any aspect of an institution's programs, operations, management, or strategic planning. The support or service members can provide can include anything they are willing to do: raise money, be good-will ambassadors to external constituencies, arrange field trips or guest speakers, bake cookies for staff recognition dinners. They can do virtually anything they and the staff agree to, except make decisions on policy. Some committees provide service, some advice, some both.

• *. . . to an institution or one of its subunits.*

This last defining characteristic is somewhat arbitrary but relates more to the scope of this report than to the general subject of advisory committees. Advisory groups have become very popular at all levels of state and national education policy making. For example:

- A statewide collaboration among teacher preparation institutions in West Virginia includes representatives of all public and private teacher preparation institutions and makes recommendations to the state board (Childress 1984).
- The vocational education system has a national advisory committee, statewide councils in each state, and tens of thousands of committees at the institutional and program levels (Walters 1986).
- The National Advisory Committee on Black Higher Education and Black Colleges and Universities (1982) offers recommendations on financial aid, research and teaching assistantships, standardized testing, the switch from a two-year to a four-year college, and other issues pertaining to the target population.
- A statewide committee in New York synthesizes research and makes recommendations to social service agencies on how to better meet the needs of immigrants of African descent (New York Governor's 1988).

These advisory boards to arms of the federal or state governments or to national or regional agencies have some elements in common with the institutional advisory committees addressed in this report, but many of the circumstances differ. For example, state councils on vocational education

ypically hire staff and might have their own executive direc-
or, resulting in very different functional dynamics than, say,
an advisory committee to the dean of business at a university.
The primary focus in this report is on the local level—advisory
committees working with institutions of higher education or
with specific programs within them.

Institutional and Programmatic Advisory Committees

Institutional advisory committees can be one of two general
categories: *broad-based* (institutionwide) program or discipline *specific*. An institution of higher education might have
one committee serving in a general advisory capacity to the
whole institution plus as many as 50 different advisory groups
serving programs or subunits (Cuninggim 1985). Campuswide
advisory committees might engage in a range of activities:

- Marshall University's advisory committee is responsible
  for a broad spectrum of activities, including academic
  standards; curriculum development and evaluation; faculty recruitment, development, promotion, and tenure;
  health services; career services; teacher education; and
  minority students (Mayer 1981).
- Many colleges tap the expertise of alumni and parents
  with public relations backgrounds to help administrators
  focus on specific areas like marketing and public relations
  (Callaghan 1986).
- The president of Ramapo College carefully picked a team
  of corporate leaders whom he taps for help in strategic
  planning. He uses the group for advice about capital planning, the college's land holdings, and issues that Ramapo's trustees or its fund-raising group cannot deal with
  (Scott 1988).
- All of the California community colleges were required
  to set up campuswide committees to address specific
  adaptations needed to accommodate students with hand-
  icaps (Baker and Ostertag 1981).
- Valencia Community College dramatically increased its
  enrollment of African-Americans by setting up an advisory
  committee to address the issue. The committee started
  by hosting several promotional activities that brought the
  college into the African-American community, and it has
  continued to work on issues of recruiting and retaining
  people of color (Valencia Community College 1980).

- Some small liberal arts colleges use advisory committees for "environmental scanning" as part of comprehensive strategic planning (Popovics and Jonas 1992).

Programmatic or discipline-based advisory committees might address more specific topics:

- An advisory committee in technical communications provides a two-way exchange between faculty and members of the business community (Brockman 1982).
- The dean of the College of Business Administration at Ohio State University uses an advisory group to "link the academic community to the external community," drawing on advisers as mentors and role models for students, sources of speakers, and help for faculty to restructure the curriculum and to keep their own skills upgraded (Silver 1988).
- Alumni aged 60 and over at the University of Toronto serve on an advisory committee that provides input into the gerontology program and service as guest speakers and resources. Some members volunteer in the library and as guides for campus tours (Gleberzon 1981).
- An advisory committee for teacher preparation at the University of Wisconsin at Milwaukee helps focus courses and checks their relevance, and suggests ideas for faculty research (Schug 1982).
- The communications department of Central Missouri State University uses its advisory committees primarily to help keep its programs up to date with the changing employment market but also benefits from the availability of contacts for student internships, evaluation concerning the programs, and enhanced overall credibility (Winsor et al. 1992).

A nonprofit organization's large alcoholism program might have, in addition to its umbrella advisory committee, a committee for each of its several specific programs. Other groups might set up client advisory committees for targeted feedback on specific programs (Ibrahim et al. 1987). Many community colleges have committees established for each curricular area (Garrity 1984) or for clusters of related courses or activities (Brawer and Gates 1981) or for special functions, such as cooperative education (Hartley 1980) or the college bookstore (Salsini 1986).

The diverse support and advice advisory committees provide underscore the tremendous potential they have for connecting colleges and universities to the outside world.

WHY ESTABLISH AN ADVISORY COMMITTEE?

Colleges and universities interact in many ways with their environments: attracting students and then placing them in jobs or further schooling, maintaining accreditation, attracting teachers, administrators, and other staff, raising funds, purchasing supplies, erecting buildings, disposing of waste products, among others. Nonprofit organizations, too, must interact with their environments—securing funding, attracting and maintaining high-caliber staff, acquiring facilities, marketing services, providing quality services, and adapting to a changing economic, social, and political environment. Virtually any significant decision made by a group, academic institution, or program affects how it interacts with its environment; each needs to respond to a variety of constituencies. Yet most decisions are made by faculty, administrators, and staff inside the unit.

Advisory committees can provide valuable assistance for "boundary personnel."

An advisory committee provides an opportunity to facilitate some exchange between the organization and its environment. A key ingredient in an organization's approach to its environment, it could be part of a larger approach to strategic planning and/or total quality management. Advisory committees can provide valuable assistance for, and in some cases complement, the "boundary personnel," those individuals who help conduct the organization's business with the rest of the world.

Help in Interacting with the Environment
A useful framework identifies six roles that boundary personnel must fill: *representing* the organization to external constituencies, *scanning and monitoring* the environment for potential problems or opportunities, *processing and gatekeeping* information that comes into the organization, *transacting and overseeing* the exchange of resources between the organization and its environment, *linking and coordinating* with other institutions, and *protecting* the organization from external threats (Miles 1980).

Advisory committees for and within institutions of higher education can support, and in some cases conduct, most of these boundary activities. With regard to the key role they can play in representation, "One of the most important purposes for which advisory councils are established is public relations, the systematic effort to portray the institution so as to elicit feelings of admiration and warmth . . . , to build good will" (Cuninggim 1985, p. 12). While deans or academic departments frequently set up advisory committees with the "notion of bringing professionals to campus for such purposes as policy guidance and fund-raising, . . . as vehicles for scanning and monitoring, these committees represent expanded channels, with the capacity for processing messages of greater bandwidth and bringing multiple perspectives to bear on current issues" (Gratz and Salem 1989, p. 99). In their transacting roles, members of advisory committees might be involved with raising funds, finding jobs for graduates and co-op jobs for current students, and recruiting personnel (Corley 1988).

Advisory committee members frequently represent companies and community organizations with which colleges or universities wish to be more closely linked. More general linking and coordinating roles of advisory committees include steps to "improve the school's relationships in several crucial directions: with other schools in and outside the university, with the university's central administration, with church or state, depending on institutional sponsorship, with various community agencies near and far, with professional organizations, and with sister institutions wherever" (Cuninggim 1985, pp. 13–14). And advisory committees are often seen as a way of protecting a program or a school, by developing powerful stakeholders in the community and by coopting potential critics (Office of the State Director 1987). The only one of the six categories mentioned earlier in which advisory committees do not usually play a major role is processing and gatekeeping, which is largely an internal function, although committees can play a role in suggesting policies that can improve that process.

Advisory Committees in Institutional Planning and Improvement
By helping colleges and universities to open up their environments, advisory committees have the great potential to help them be more responsive to the challenges of today's world. Driven, in many cases, by declining enrollments and/or diminishing budgets, institutions find themselves under increased pressure to do more with less. At the same time, the demands and expectations for responsiveness and accountability have increased, requiring greater interaction with the world outside the Ivory Tower (Bok 1982; Seymour 1989) and leading to increased interest over the last ten years in strategic planning (Cope 1987; G. Keller 1983) and, more re-

cently, total quality management (TQM) (Chaffee and Sherr 1992). Both approaches help organizations cope with and respond to an uncertain and changing external environment. Strategic planning promotes a clarity of mission and self-renewal that provides the best positioning for the institution; TQM urges organizations to listen to their "customers" (both inside and outside the organization) and design high-quality processes to best meet their needs. The growth of interest in advisory committees shares its roots with strategic planning and TQM. Advisory committees can provide mechanisms at all levels of higher education to help improve communication and interaction with the outside world. In conjunction with a strategic plan or total quality approach, they can be key elements in renewing and revitalizing an institution.

Practical Reasons to Establish an Advisory Committee
Setting up an advisory committee requires time and effort, and involvement in one could bring additional headaches for management. Why, in the absence of any external compulsion, would an individual staff or faculty member or administrator voluntarily seek to work with an advisory committee?

The simplest and most compelling reason is the sincere belief that by welcoming and using input from a variety of perspectives, the institution or program will be improved. A more specific motivation, however, might be developing or tuning a program to ensure the relevance of its content and the appropriateness of its delivery. In Oklahoma, for example, two home economics specialists planned the statewide in-service sessions required of all home economics teachers by setting up an advisory committee comprised of members of the target population to assess needs (Cadwalader and Daugherty 1989). Similarly, the nontraditional programs at the University College of the University of Richmond (Virginia) use an advisory committee made up of the professionals the college serves (Larson 1990).

Another type of targeting might be to use an advisory panel to capture the input of some significant third party. A career training program (whether for a career as a welder or a bank president) might want to include input from potential employers of its graduates. A teacher preparation program might want input from administrators as well as experienced teachers (Schug 1982).

Sometimes multiple constituencies are interested in influencing the organization. An advisory committee can hear from different constituencies and balance different forces that might exist in the community, freeing staff to address problems and issues they are paid to address (Ibrahim et al. 1987). Advisory committees can also provide important access to jobs and internships for students (Cochran, Phelps, and Cochran 1980; Winsor et al. 1992).

An organization might use an advisory committee as a form of outreach to an underrepresented population. Valencia Community College set up such an advisory committee to attract more African-American students to the campus. Initially comprised of 40 of the African-American community's leaders, the Committee of Forty staged several successful publicity events, helping increase the college's African-American population significantly. The committee's role evolved to addressing the issues of people of color on campus (Valencia Community College 1980).

An advisory committee can help a program gain legitimacy in a community. Sometimes social service agencies attempt to deliver services but find that potential clients are subtly discouraged from participating by members of their particular community. An advisory committee can help forge the links that can lead to sanction and acceptance (Dyer and Williams 1991). In an academic setting, the communications advisory committees at Central Missouri State University increased the program's credibility in the community (Winsor et al. 1992).

Setting up an advisory committee can also add clout and legitimacy to a program or institution. Within an organization, an advisory committee can bolster the staff's position when approaching the college administration on issues or with specific requests (Salsini 1986). Advisory committees are particularly important for nontraditional programs, such as programs for students with mild dyslexia or special support services for minority students, struggling for resources in a large university (Welch 1989). Advisory groups, in these cases comprised primarily of faculty from traditional departments, "provide the university community with a sense of a program's accountability and credibility" (p. 73). Exposing potential and actual critics to a closer view of the program can convert them into valuable supporters.

Advisory committees can be effective political allies in the larger community as well. For example, the University of California at San Diego faced a potential controversy over retaining its tax-exempt status for undeveloped land it owned. Its community advisory council explored the issue, held several public hearings, and recommended the properties be retained with their tax-exempt status. "If the university had reached the same conclusion after conducting its own study, the decision might not have been accepted" (Rowland 1980, p. 61). The opposite, of course, can also occur: An advisory committee might explore the issues and recommend against the program's interests.*

By involving potential detractors, advisory committees can provide powerful political tools to defuse opposition (Cochran, Phelps, and Cochran 1980). An advisory committee can also augment the work of the governing board, for it can perform tasks that are important to the institution but might not require the governing board's full attention. And advisory committees can serve as a way to help groom future board members (Axelrod 1991; Laney 1984).

Factors Contributing to the Formation of Advisory Committees

Certain circumstances increase the likelihood of the voluntary establishment of advisory committees. The attitudes of faculty, staff, and administrators toward advisory groups are not static, responding to changing personalities, needs, and perceptions. Some managers are by temperament and style more open to broader input than others, seeking additional outside expertise and advice (Scott 1988). An institution might set up or revitalize an advisory committee in response to such a leader—or it might dismantle or let lapse one after such an individual leaves.

The openness to outside input might be more than personal; it might be part of a corporate culture or subculture. The continuing education division of one community college, for example, had a responsive, externally focused approach to education ("continuing education mentality") that made setting up and *listening* to advisory committees an important piece of its subculture (Teitel 1991). Administrators had some success in exporting the process to the rest of the faculty,

---

*Comments from an anonymous reviewer.

which at first had minimal interest in establishing and maintaining active advisory committees.

"Voluntary" advisory committees might be set up in response to real or perceived external pressures. One might be established as a preemptive strike against a pressure group an organization senses might be forming, or perhaps because some regulatory authority might be considering requiring outside input. If the community is changing demographically in ways that are not reflected in the governing board or the staff, an organization might set up an advisory committee to get input from different segments of the population and to defuse potential criticism or regulation.

In other cases, advisory committees, even though they are not required per se, satisfy some externally placed requirements. For example, although accrediting agencies might not require advisory boards, they could require evidence of external input and evaluation that advisory committee can provide. With regard to the increase in advisory councils in teacher preparation, "most councils appear to be closely tied to [National Council for Accreditation of Teacher Education] standards for accreditation. Although NCATE standards do not require a council, the councils have apparently been the structure most frequently used to meet the standard for 'governance of basic programs'" (Dearmin 1982, p. 3). Faculty in other fields note that an active advisory committee is seen as a plus in gaining accreditation (Winsor et al. 1992).

Changing Needs for Advisory Committees
At different points in its development, a program might have different attitudes toward advisory committees. Many theorists argue that an organization's need for input and output varies substantially during its creation, transformation, and decline (Hannah and Freeman 1978; Kimberly 1981). Similarly, the roles of advisory committees can change over time as a result of different needs dictated by the organization's life cycle. Institutions might want high levels of advice at some points, high levels of support and service at others, and both or neither at still other points in their development.

Starting a new program is a natural time to seek input from an advisory committee: "The group can assist in validating the need for the program, help locate resources and instructional personnel, and promote the program within the community" (Gross 1980, p. 11). Often committees are estabished as part of the improvement or expansion of a program. The use of advisory groups is particularly likely if revitalizing a program requires bringing it up to date with changes made in the outside world in, say, computer science (American Association 1989). A "newly established or revitalized advisory committee can do much to help the older program maintain its responsiveness to changing conditions and needs of the community it serves" (Gross 1980, p. 11). Although this statement is generally true, institutional staff might be more likely to recognize these benefits and establish an advisory committee when a program is in trouble (Reynolds 1979). College or university administrators who desire a change in a program's direction might seek to set up advisory committees or reformulate them for new roles as a way to get more input in shaping the programs. Community college administrators involved in a major transformation of their institution used the influence of outsiders to bring about institutional change (Teitel 1991). One administrator boasted of his success in "cracking" seven programs through the advisory committees: The committees were reconstituted and helped transform the programs into being more responsive to the needs of business and industry in the area. One must bear in mind, however, that faculty and staff might not always perceive committee members who help bring about dramatic change in a positive light and that those committee members might need to be replaced by others.

Circumstances that require greater collaboration with others can also prompt the use of an advisory committee. A new teacher preparation program at Emporia State University, for example, required unusual collaboration with schools and with different segments of the university (1985). It used an advisory committee as a coordinating mechanism.

Advisory committees can also fill new roles during transitions. In one organization, until the director resigned, the advisory committee was very pleasant and worked with the organization on small projects but was never really involved with major issues. But when the director resigned, the committee began to be more active and more involved in working with the new director, providing her with some continuity.*

Teitel 1991, interview notes.

Just as an institution's needs can change over time, advisory committees themselves evolve and might need to play different roles as the program stabilizes or develops. Sometimes advisory committees meet more frequently when a program is started but then have a less clearly defined role and lose momentum. Consequently, committees should revisit their purpose periodically in collaboration with staff, administration, and faculty as a way to monitor the group's performance (Axelrod 1991).

External Pressures

Although no other sector's requirement to use advisory committees is as clear, long, and comprehensive as federally funded vocational-technical programs and the schools and colleges that house them, other programs and institutions face increasing external mandates—from funders, from those grant ing licenses, or from accrediting agencies, for example. Programs might face an external mandate because the overall organization has decided to require particular subunits to establish advisory groups. For example, a university might demand advisory groups for its programs or collegiate subunits

The primary reason for external mandates is the belief that input from outside the organization will contribute to better programs more suited to the needs of target populations or society at large. Advisory committees are seen as ways to ensure accountability, relevance, and efficient use of state, local, or federal funds (Dyer and Williams 1991; Gross 1980), to provide a check on the way money is spent (Axelrod 1991)

Pressure often exists, implicitly or explicitly, to have agencies, schools, and colleges respond to new clienteles. Advisory committees or community advisory boards, comprised of members reflecting a specific demographic composition, can be mandated as a way to try to ensure that responsiveness (Ibrahim et al. 1987).

In some circumstances, an advisory committee can be a mechanism to promote collaboration between and among organizations. An applicant for funding might be asked to provide evidence of an advisory committee comprised of potentially linked organizations as a precondition for funding.

The next section explores what happens when advisory committees are mandated.

THE VOCATIONAL EDUCATION STORY: A Case Study in Mandated Advisory Committees

When advisory committees are mandated—whether by external funders, accreditation groups, or higher levels of administration—a number of special issues emerge. The history of advisory committees in vocational education provides a case study of what can happen when advisory groups are externally mandated. In comparison to other sectors, where advisory committees are more recently being mandated, vocational education has the longest history (almost a century) and is the best documented (more than 40 percent of the documents in an ERIC search of "advisory committees in education" refer to vocational or technical programs). But the issues that surface in a study of vocational advisory committees bear on other sectors. Three themes are particularly relevant:

1. The growing use of mandated advisory committees and the expansion of their roles;
2. The history of advisory committees' perceived ineffectiveness; and
3. The efforts to improve advisory committees' effectiveness by providing program and institution staff with instructional advice and appeals to their institutional self-interest.

The Growing Use of Advisory Committees

Using advisory committees to shape the policies and curricula of vocational education dates back to the beginning of the 20th century. Even before the Smith-Hughes Act of 1917 provided the first federal money for vocational education, the National Society for the Promotion of Industrial Education was on record urging that any federal program be administered by a board representing employers, labor, and education and that those boards be required to appoint advisory committees to assist them in their work (Hawkins, Prosser, and Wright 1951). From their early use to shape national decisions, advisory committees have permeated all segments and levels of vocational education and spread from national to state to local levels, following progressively increased mandates in federal legislation. The National Advisory Council was mandated in the Vocational Education Act of 1963, state advisory councils in the 1968 amendment to that act, and local committees in the 1976 amendment. The Carl Perkins Act of 1984 added greater specificity to the requirements, detailing composition of the committees and clarifying responsibilities on all levels (Corley 1988). It calls for two common types of institutional advisory committees: the craft- or subject-specific committee, and the more general occupational or vocational advisory committee, which might be comprised of people from a variety of different vocational areas (Finch and McGough 1982).

The primary focus of early federal and state legislation requiring the use of advisory committees in vocational and technical education was the concern that graduates of such programs be prepared to meet the needs of the job. Consequently, early advisory committees included craftsmen and potential employers. By the middle of the century, the purpose of advisory committees had expanded beyond curricular input to issues of inclusion: In the mid-1950s, the group to be included was organized labor to defuse potential suspicions of vocational education (King 1960). More recently, the membership of advisory committees has been specified to include both sexes, people of varying ages and ethnic backgrounds, and representatives of a variety of community agencies in an effort to ensure access and to include diverse segments of the population in vocational and technical education (Corley 1988).

The History of Perceived Ineffectiveness
The perception that many of the mandated vocational education advisory groups were ineffective paper committees that did not even meet appears to be almost as old as the committees themselves. In 1939, for example, over 1,300 local craft advisory committees for specific local programs were reported in 40 states, and 26 states reported provisions for general state-level advisory committees. Yet:

> *The difference between the number of states having provisions in their plans and the number of states having active advisory committees at work was so great as to cause adverse comment on the part of organized labor. Charges were made that the provision in state plans was "window dressing"* (Hawkins, Prosser, and Wright 1951, p. 427).

More recently, many state-level councils on vocational education have published how-to books and pamphlets that indicate the persistence of this problem. Common in the prefaces of such books is the acknowledgment that amid the proliferation of advisory committees are many that function ineffectively or do not even meet: "Despite all the emphasis and support for the formation and use of advisory councils, they have been less effective than one would hope. They frequently exist largely on paper and meet informally and irregularly if at all" (Office of the State Director 1987). In one study, one-sixth of the individuals who were identified by schools as members of advisory committees had no knowledge that they were even serving in that capacity (Massachusetts Dept. of Education 1985). A study in South Carolina found that most of the 1,000 respondents who were members of advisory committees reported that, in their view, their committees had no impact on the programs they served. Seventy percent of those surveyed reported their committees had had no recommendations implemented (Oswald 1984). Because ineffective advisory committees cannot properly be blamed on the committees or their members, a long history exists of efforts to change the attitudes and skills of the faculty, staff, or administration responsible for setting them up.

Efforts to Improve Advisory Committees' Effectiveness
To help vocational educators and school and college administrators handle what for many is an unfamiliar challenge, the instructional handbooks many states have issued describe everything from the selection of members and possible agendas for first meetings to thank you letters and recognition ceremonies for the committee members (see, e.g., Maryland State Advisory Council 1984; Nebraska State Advisory Council 1982; Office of the State Director 1987; Oklahoma State Council 1988).

In attempting to promote the use of advisory committees, the state councils offer more than just instructions on the number of mandated meetings and hints on running meetings. They have tried to overcome the perceived reluctance of local educators by appealing to their own self-interest. The handbooks, in addition to spelling out federal requirements, highlight other political and economic benefits of maintaining an advisory committee. Typical are the guidelines from the state director for vocational education in Hawaii (1987), which, in addition to stressing the obvious advantages of having a mechanism for keeping the curricula relevant and providing guest speakers, field trips, internships, and job placements for graduates, suggests that businesspeople become

The handbooks have tried to ovecome the perceived reluctance of local educators by appealing to their own self-interest.

"stakeholders" in the school or college. The report suggests that the "business sector will be more likely to offer technical advice and assist in fund-raising if [it feels it is] involved, recognized as contributors, and will be benefactors of the program" (p. 4).

The report cites other gains that might be appealing to program administrators and staff. An advisory committee, for example, can lobby with school or college administrators to acquire state-of-the-art equipment without being subject to the suspicion that such a request from a teacher might raise. It can also be useful for "derailing detractors of a program." Offering a voice through the committee will either involve or silence the critic (Office of the State Director 1987).

Issues and Implications Involving Mandated Advisory Committees

Although no other sectors of higher education have had as much experience with mandated advisory committees as vocational education, many of the issues described in that literature are broadly applicable. In other settings, particularly those that are publicly funded, advisory committees are increasingly required for accountability or for relevance and to make sure programs meet the needs of target populations. Further, ample anecdotal evidence suggests that the rest of higher education and the nonprofit organizations have their share of underfunctioning advisory committees (Axelrod 1991; Thompson 1984). The vocational education story underscores an important point about mandatory advisory committees: For mandates to work, institutional representatives need support and guidelines and need to be convinced that an advisory committee is not only in the interests of their programs, but also worth the time and effort.

The necessity for guidance in establishing and maintaining a mandated advisory committee

Often a requirement for an advisory committee comes with no clear definition or guidance. The California law that mandated citizen advisory committees for programs and services for handicapped students "stated simply that an advisory committee must be established and that the committee must be [comprised] of representatives determined by program need" (Baker and Ostertag 1981, p. 1). A review of the process by which the allied health accreditation board began to require advisory committees draws parallels to the rise of mandated committees in vocational education (Gross 1980), noting that although the accreditation board for respiratory therapy "required" advisory committees in its 1972 guides, it provided neither guidelines nor penalties for any programs if they failed to comply. In 1978, the board announced that reaccreditation and certification of new programs would be jeopardized by the lack of a committee, but at no point in the process of mandating advisory committees did the accreditation board issue any guidelines that went beyond composition and number of meetings annually. The lack of readily available education or training materials potentially undercuts the very purpose of a mandated advisory committee:

> *The educator who is required to develop and maintain an advisory committee for conformance with [a] . . . requirement is in a dilemma. He has to respond to these external forces but likely without the necessary understanding or guidance to achieve the final goals of such standards, which are program improvement and quality assurance. This situation has led to perhaps one of the greatest concerns mentioned in the literature, unused or misused advisory groups* (Gross 1980, p. 23).

This lack of guidance is even more pervasive in other sectors of higher education, which have less access to the type of instructional advice available to those in vocational education. One of the few handbooks available (although for nonprofit organizations) warns of the drains of dysfunctional advisory committees and stresses the need to educate staff in how to work with and use committees effectively (Axelrod 1991). The dearth of other literature is highlighted in a university president's urging other presidents and deans to start actively using advisory committees; his citation for some specific advice is from a manual published by the Indiana State Advisory Council on Vocational Education (Laney 1984).

The necessity to be convinced of a committee's usefulness

The collected wisdom of the instructional books from the vocational education sector stresses that effective advisory committees need "proper guidance" from the program staff, yet it would be faulty to presume that program faculty understand "the underlying principles on which the advisory committee concept is built." The consequences could be dire—exactly the kind of paper committee external agencies do not want: "An advisory group developed with an incomplete understanding of its role and purpose will likely conform to the letter of the law or standard but just as likely not accomplish its real purpose" (Gross 1980, p. 24).

As a practical matter, accreditation agencies and other external sources of funding have few or no means of assessing whether advisory committees are genuinely providing input to a program, whether they are rubber stamps, or whether they exist largely on paper. Unless advisory committee members themselves are assessed periodically (Massachusetts Dept. of Education 1985, 1986), external parties must rely on the reporting of meeting dates and membership from the institutions themselves. The weak enforcement arm underscores the importance, from the point of view of the mandating authority, of trying to change attitudes so that institutional representatives truly value input. The key to it is having organizations mesh external goals with internal ones. "Many . . . organizations have been successful in expanding the role of these 'required' groups from performing exclusively for the benefit of an external party to vehicles that genuinely contribute to management and governance" (Axelrod 1991, p. 2).

The next section explores this critical change in institutional representatives' attitude as one of the determinants of advisory committees' direction and effectiveness.

ATTITUDES AND EXPECTATIONS OF DEANS, DIRECTORS, AND STAFF

Many deans, directors, staff, and faculty members find the extra effort they put into working with an advisory committee time well spent. But that involvement with an advisory committee has its down side, and, despite the benefits, some institutional representatives approach advisory groups with caution—or at least with some ambivalence. Administrators, faculty, and staff play such key roles in setting up and maintaining advisory committees that their attitudes and expectations—especially the depth of their desire for the committee's input—are important determinants of an advisory committee's effectiveness. If they do not find that the benefits of an advisory committee outweigh its costs, they are unlikely to provide the critical support necessary for an effective committee.

Clarifying Advisory Committees' Roles and Expectations

Active advisory committees bring complications along with their many benefits. Even when committees focus primarily on service tasks like fund-raising, public relations, or employee appreciation dinners, working with them takes time and energy—another nine or so people to work with, to keep engaged, productive, and happy.* When the committee's work includes input and advice, additional complications can arise, frequently over how much advice is desirable and appropriate. Much of the instructional literature on establishing and maintaining an advisory committee focuses on clarifying the amount of input expected from such a committee (Cochran, Phelps, and Cochran 1980; Corley 1988; Oen 1985). Defining the scope of an advisory committee's input is difficult. On the one hand, school or college administrators should not:

> Initiate programs without, at least, "consulting" with [their] advisory council; take action within the realm of the designated functions of the advisory council without consulting the group; or ignore the council's recommendations without, at least, an adequate and well-articulated explanation (Office of the State Director 1987, pp. 30–31).

---

*Teitel 1992, interview notes.

On the other hand, even as they are told to be responsive to the advisory committee's input, educators are also told not to:

Permit councils to become "administrative" in their functions and exercise authority beyond their legitimate mandate (Office of the State Director 1987, p. 31).

Defining exactly what is "legitimate" input is a challenging task, subject to many different points of view and having many ramifications. How detailed a response should staff prepare for committee members? How much access to information should committee members have? How far in advance should members have agendas? Should members be asked to respond to a lengthy report they have just received? Drawing the line is not simple. Confusion about what is appropriate "advice" combines with the ambivalence some educators have about outside input and leads to a broad range in the type and level of advice offered by advisory committees and accepted by administrators.

The Spectrum of Advisory Committees

Some programs and institutions are successful in finding the appropriate balance between too much and too little input. They have developed effective advisory committees—defined here as committees that meet regularly and work together to provide advice and/or support that contributes significantly to a program's or institution's improvement. Even within this definition of effectiveness, however, the committee's role and how much advice it offers vary. Some advisory committees provide important support and service but little or no advice. Committees that do give advice range from those whose focus and direction are carefully directed by the staff, administration, or faculty to those with significant independence in addressing a wide range and scope of topics. Again, the attitude of institutional representatives is critical in shaping the committee's focus and scope.

Other committees are unsuccessful in finding the right balance. In some, the advisory groups overfunction, providing advice where none is wanted and getting involved in affairs that should be left for program directors, staff, or faculty. Several types of committees operate at the other end of the spectrum and are unused or underused. Some exist in name only and have never met; others have one organizational meeting and then exist for years on paper. Some committees meet once or twice annually, for largely ceremonial purposes. Others are largely a collection of advisers who might individually provide advice or support but whose committee rarely, if ever, meets. Even though such committees are defined here as underfunctioning, many deans, directors, faculty, and staff are entirely satisfied with them. The committees that rarely meet might nominally satisfy the requirements of an external mandate, they take little effort to maintain, and, an institutional representative might argue, they are ready to be galvanized into action if needed. Ceremonial committees also take relatively little effort and could provide important symbolic support in the larger community or for the staff. Those who use a collection of advisers as individuals can receive input without the hassles that can arise from a more active and cohesive advisory group.

Another common type of advisory committee that also underuses its members is a rubber stamp committee. In such a committee, administrators, faculty, or staff resolve the question of how much input to ask of the advisory committee by bringing important matters for the committee's consideration, but only after the decisions are substantially or entirely made. Although it might feel like a good balance point for institutional representatives between giving the committee too much or too little input, it is probably the greatest source of disgruntled committee members.

The Rubber Stamp Syndrome

Members usually accept an invitation to join an advisory committee to provide advice and input, pleased and even proud to be recognized for their "acknowledged expertise" in an area (Light 1982). On some committees, however, they find themselves without the information needed or a real opportunity to have an impact. Many advisers from industry complain about their role on vocational advisory committees where they find themselves rubber stamps whose genuine advice is unappreciated and evidently unwanted (Cochran, Phelps, and Cochran 1980; Rice and Buescher 1984). As disgruntled committee members put it:

I attended three meetings, all of which turned out to be social dinners. The teachers in charge . . . did not want our

*input, never gave us a chance to comment in our areas.
. . . I do not need [and] will [not] waste my time going to
dinner meetings and socials* (Massachusetts Dept. of Education 1985, pp. 8–9).

*Basically we as a committee serve as a front. We do what
the administration wants. We are told only enough to feel
comfortable in okaying what they want. . . . I don't feel that
anyone wants real input from the committee* (Massachusetts
Dept. of Education 1986, p. 9).

Some advisory committees really want their members'
input. Others feel like show and tell, letting the members see
only what they want to be seen.* When the staff does not want
substantial input into how they were planning to do their
work, they might try to use the committee for surface activities
like forums or hearings, all the time knowing exactly what
they want, creating a frustrating experience for members.†

Disgruntled advisory committee members have only a few
options: They can fight to have a voice and to make it heard,
they can resign (quietly or with a public show of displeasure),
or they can drift away, attending fewer and fewer meetings
(Axelrod 1991).

In one case, an advisory committee chose to fight for influence in shaping a program (Dahl 1986). The principal who
was asked to serve on an advisory group charged with considering improvements in a university's educational administration program was at first flattered, then disappointed when
university faculty "became protective of their program and
talked at length on the reasons that certain elements of the
[planning] document should be retained" (p. 2). When meetings began to be taken up with lengthy discussions by the
faculty, other members of the committee gave up, citing pressures of their own jobs and a lack of confidence that they
would have any impact. It looked as though the committee
would dwindle into insignificance. But when a faculty member maneuvered to abolish the committee, the members
rebelled and unanimously (and successfully) pushed to continue and to be heard. In retrospect, the principal is pleased
to have had an impact and glad to have asserted herself but
also understands "why the professors could not let go of

---

*Teitel 1992, interview notes.
†Teitel 1991, interview notes.

their ideas. They belonged to them, they were taught these concepts, and they were not about to surrender their turf without a fight" (p. 2).

The frustration of committee members is a key factor in contributing to poorly functioning committees (Axelrod 1991). To illustrate, one hypothetical committee member resigns in disillusionment from his role as a member of a public television station's community advisory board:

> *He agreed to serve on this committee with high hopes for becoming a productive member and contributing to the station's public affairs campaign devoted to celebrating cultural diversity . . . , [but] he still does not understand what the station is all about and what is expected of him individually. He had been excited about the prospect of applying his experience as a successful marketing executive to the station, [but] he has seen no real opportunity to contribute. Furthermore, [he] suspects that the community advisory board was established merely to fulfill a requirement by the university licensee for this station* (Axelrod 1991, pp. 11–12).

It is hard to estimate how widespread the rubber stamp syndrome is. Authors of instructional books and articles often talk vaguely about how advisory committees are "less effective than one would hope" (Office of the State Director 1987, p. 2) or about "the growing gap between expectations and performance" (Axelrod 1991, p. 3). Others conclude that "advisory committees are often dysfunctional" (Cochran, Phelps, and Cochran 1980, p. xix). In even more blunt terms:

> *All vocational technical education institutions pay at least lip service to the use of advisory committees [comprised] of "outsiders" who help guide their separate occupation programs. As a matter of fact, the reality of the situation is that advisory committees frequently operate with a minimum of effectiveness, or do not operate at all* (Light 1982, p. 1).

How Much Input Do Institutional Representatives Really Want?

Is serving primarily as a rubber stamp necessarily bad? After all, the staff or faculty or administration knows more about day-to-day operations than outsiders. Perhaps it makes sense for them to formulate policy and then seek approval from the committee.

Who judges effectiveness? If members of the advisory committee do not get their way, is the committee ineffective? Must the advice be accepted for the committee to be effective? Instead, perhaps merely raising issues and subsequently discussing them would serve to clarify issues for those who run a program or plant seeds that bear fruit much later. Do those outcomes make the committee effective or not?*

One cause of the rubber stamp syndrome is the difficulty in finding how much advice is appropriate. Perhaps advisory committees are underused in part because educators do not *understand* the value of an active advisory committee or because they (along with committee members) are unclear about what the role of the committee is (Cochran, Phelps, and Cochran 1980). While an organization might see a committee's potential "to help the staff and board do wondrous things, [members] are often ambivalent about what they really want them to do or how they can help them do it" (Axelrod 1991, p. 27). Others note that some faculty and administrators do not *want* the input or fear that they will have to implement a recommendation they do not agree with (King 1960, p. 55). Some believe that, as highly trained experts, they do not need to seek the advice of others (Schug 1982) or that the locus of control should remain within the institution. It might be "inertia, a sense that learning can [occur only] within a school, not knowing how to organize such a group, and the assumption that community representatives are not interested" (Gross 1980, p. 14).

But an advisory committee that contributes a large amount of advice and help presents a number of challenges for program management. While an advisory committee might be helpful for activities like fund-raising and employee appreciation events and occasionally as a sounding board on new initiatives, one might avoid asking the committee for real advice about central issues for two reasons.

First is a question of information. The organization would have to spend much time and effort to bring committee members up to speed, to educate them well enough so they can provide meaningful feedback. Second, even if that

---

*Comments from an anonymous reviewer.

*effort were made and the organization would get a more
complete picture than just its internal decision making provides, it also would make administrators' jobs more complicated, because they then would have to deal with conflicting information. And if administrators do not agree,
how would committee members feel if their advice were
not followed?**

In addition to making life more complicated for administrators, having an active advisory committee that provides
large amounts of advice implicitly opens up the decision-
making process to a greater level of scrutiny than some might
want. Even if a director or dean makes clear that the advisory
committee's input will be one of many factored into a decision, he or she still has to report back to the committee on
the decision and what influenced it. According to one administrator, explaining the control of a program director over that
program's advisory board:

*The agendas were all created in advance and the committee
could do nothing but move through them, orchestrated by
the program director. She was afraid they might ask her to
do something that she didn't want to do or didn't know how
to do, and she made sure not to give them a chance.†*

These tensions between staff and committee can be exacerbated in some settings where committees are more likely
comprised of recipients of services, who might be more critical (Ibrahim et al. 1987). Having an advisory committee that
really gives advice will have an effect on the organization's
style of management. The program leader's personal style is
tied to whether he or she finds advisory committees "an outright pain in the neck to be avoided at all cost" or "a decided
asset" (Borden 1984, pp. II-1, II-2).

Institutions should decide what they want from their advisory committees:

*[An advisory] committee moves between two poles. At one
extreme is a committee informed only of what the school*

*Teitel 1991, interview notes.
†Teitel 1992, interview notes.

wants it to know or even allows it to know. At the other is a committee charged to learn, to investigate, what the school itself wants to know but doesn't have the personnel, capacity, or judgment to find out. Between them lies a wide variance. The implication is clear: The committee is either an active one or a passive one (Laney 1984, p. 31).

Some will argue that this picture overdraws the choices, not leaving room, for instance, for an advisory committee that is appropriately focused on a specific topic. Even though the issue is not as clear-cut as this description, it does pinpoint one of the central issues contributing to effective and active advisory committees. And the attitudes of upper management are key: Effective use of an advisory committee requires the commitment of the institution and the program to the use of advisory committees and an interest in the input they provide (Parry-Hill 1981, p. 2; see also Light 1982; Rice and Buescher 1984). "The value and use of an advisory council can vary widely, depending on how much the administration and board genuinely seek community involvement in identifying and improving secondary and adult training" (Carroll 1981, p. iii).

The lack of openness on the part of the institutional representatives is likely to doom a committee's input to irrelevance unless external pressure is brought to bear, members are highly motivated to change circumstances, or a particularly powerful group dynamic develops. These factors are discussed in the next sections.

THE MOTIVATION AND COMMITMENT OF VOLUNTEERS

Advisory committees are comprised of volunteers who join and serve for a variety of complex reasons. Their motivation, type of commitment, and willingness to put time and effort into the advisory committee are key variables in defining the committee's direction and effectiveness.*

Why Do Volunteers Volunteer?
When asked, most volunteers report that their principal reason for volunteering is altruism. Since 1981, when the Gallup organization started annually asking Americans who volunteer why they do it, the most frequent response consistently has to do with the desire to help others (Brudney 1990; see also Anderson and Moore 1978). But when investigators probe farther beneath the surface, using other research methodology like intensive interviews, they discover that volunteers are rarely solely motivated by pure altruism (Ellis 1986; Smith 1981; Van Til 1988). The decision to volunteer is made after a careful analysis, either conscious or unconscious, of the costs and benefits of doing so (Schindler-Rainman and Lippitt 1975).

A useful framework for thinking about why people volunteer distinguishes between *commitment* and *motivation* (Ilsley 1990). Commitment is a deeper feeling and underlying belief structure that shapes the thinking of a potential volunteer. But commitment alone does not a volunteer make: Virtually everyone has a sense of commitment and values he or she believes in, yet most do not become volunteers. Motivation is the key ingredient that separates volunteers from nonvolunteers: "Motivation inspires one to action, whereas commitment is a deeper feeling that may or may not produce an action directly" (p. 16). To understand volunteers fully is to understand their deeper sense of commitment as well as their motivation.

Types of Commitment
Unlike motivation, commitment is *to* something—an idea, an organization, other people, a vision of the world (Ilsley 1990). The commitment of volunteers can be categorized into four types:

A useful framework for thinking about why people volunteer distinguishes between commitment *and* motivation.

---

*Because little has been written about volunteer advisory committee members, per se, this section draws on the broader literature on volunteers and volunteerism.

- *Organization-centered,* where primary loyalty is to the institution. A classic example is someone involved in an alumni association, whose links and devotion are to the college rather than, say, to higher education in general.
- *Client-centered,* in which volunteers see working for a particular organization as a means to the end of helping the ultimate recipients of the services. Examples include those involved in hospice care, in working with victims of AIDS, or in literacy programs. For many of them, at least initially, the commitment to the organization is relatively low; the organization is important mostly because of the access it provides to clients.
- *Social vision–centered,* in which volunteers see themselves as working to promote a cause or in some way working to improve the world—volunteers with political organizations and causes, such as civil rights or peace. Others with less obvious but just as strong social visions might volunteer in schools, hospitals, or other community groups. Like client-centered volunteers, their attachment to the particular organization might be relatively low.
- *Volunteer-centered,* in which volunteers' primary loyalty and commitment are to other volunteers. Many work in hospitals, where a strong sense of mutual reliance and affiliation is developed. Some begin volunteering for other reasons but remain because of the strong connections and affiliations that develop with other volunteers (Ilsley 1990, p. 35).

People do not fit neatly into one category, and commitment to one does not preclude commitment to another. Conflicts and shifts in primary allegiance develop sometimes. In fact, it is common for long-term volunteers to undergo "perspective transformations"—deep shifts in values—as a result of their volunteer activities (Ilsley 1990, p. 54).

The distinctions among the objects of commitment, while far from perfect, can be useful in thinking about the underlying values for volunteers on advisory committees. For instance, when a hypothetical vice president of marketing agrees to serve on the business advisory board at her local university, is she primarily interested in helping provide a better experience for the students or is she participating because she in an alumna and has a sense of institutional loyalty? Perhaps she is committed to a vision of ethics for business leaders and wants to influence the way students are taught. Maybe she wants to feel connected and involved with the other members of the committee. Although her underlying values might evolve over time and might even change through her involvement on the committee, the framework discussed earlier can shed some important insights into what her commitment and goals are. Imagine, for example, her reaction if the college faculty were reluctant to even discuss a proposal to infuse the teaching of ethics into their courses. If her prime commitment were to a social vision of ethics in business, her reaction might be very different from her reaction if she were motivated by institutional loyalty.

Types of Motivation

To continue the example of the hypothetical marketing vice president, other marketing vice presidents in the area undoubtedly would share her commitments (institutional loyalty or her concern about students' experience or whatever), yet they might lack sufficient motivation to agree to be on an advisory committee or to come to meetings. Three categories of motivation, besides altruism, are instrumental in understanding what motivates people to action—to volunteer or to respond favorably to a request to volunteer.

> In addition to altruism, motivations for volunteers are commonly held to include psychological benefits, such as the good feelings associated with doing something worthwhile, opportunities for personal and perhaps professional growth, and the chance to try new skills or activities in a relatively risk-free environment. . . . Research has suggested that expectation of such benefits probably plays a greater role than altruism in motivating volunteers (Ilsley 1990, p. 11).

Psychological benefits go well beyond these good feelings associated with doing something worthwhile, extending to the three basic needs in all people—the need for achievement (to accomplish something, see tangible results), for power (to have an impact), and for affiliation (to feel connected with a group) (McClelland 1976). For example, most (84 percent) of the adult volunteers in one study were motivated primarily by affiliation, only 12 percent by achievement and 4 percent by power (Henderson 1981). Volunteers in leadership positions, however, were significantly more motivated by achievement than other volunteers, volunteers on decision-making committees by a need for power (pp. 24–25).

More pragmatic needs that can be met by volunteering include opportunities for personal and professional growth or to develop and try out new skills. Many novice volunteers can readily point out the perceived benefits of volunteering.

I am not looking for a job from this, though I am hoping to expand my present job and to make contacts. I consider myself fortunate to be working here. The training is useful to me, the people are great, and I think there are some real possibilities. [I have committed my time] for a year—then I'll reassess the possibilities (Ilsley 1990, p. 23).

Practical motivations include gaining access to a facility, networking, resume building, trying out skills in a safer arena for future employment, impressing present employers in the hope of a promotion, and gaining prestige by joining a high-status group (Murk and Stephan 1990).

These motivations can change over time. Interviews with long-time volunteers (10 to 15 years) show that not only are their motivations different from those of novice volunteers, but also that their own motivations have evolved over time, often in response to the norms and expectations of the organizations for which they are volunteering (Ilsley 1990). Motivations met no longer motivate a volunteer. Some organizations lose volunteers because "they continually treat the volunteers as if they were new and had new volunteers' motives" (p. 32). In general, volunteers who continue to learn, to be recognized, and to have continuing opportunities for service, involvement, and influence are more likely to maintain their motivation. While commitments also change, they generally change more slowly because they are connected to basic values and require a greater change in perspective.

Degree of Effort

Motivations and underlying commitments prompt individuals to decide whether or not to volunteer. They also influence the magnitude and the direction of the action. At any given moment, people are willing to put more or less effort into their volunteer projects, influenced by "a myriad of internal and external characteristics. People respond to their environment on the basis of inner reflexes, impulses, perceptions, and goals, and on the basis of perceived and actual opportunities and reinforcements in the external environment" (J. Keller 1983, p. 389). Degree of effort translates into the amount of work a volunteer is willing to do. It is more volatile than motivation or commitment, far more likely to change.

To continue the example of the hypothetical vice president of marketing, when she agrees to serve on the business advisory board, she might be willing:

- To come to meetings regularly and to work in between, including preparing for the meeting and perhaps even suggesting additional tasks that she and others on the committee can perform;
- To come to meetings regularly and to prepare for them;
- To come to meetings regularly;
- To come to meetings sporadically;
- To be consulted on the telephone and be nominally listed as a member of the committee;
- To be nominally listed as a member of the committee.

The degree of effort can decrease until there is no effort at all. The last category is not to be dismissed lightly. Many people are willing to have their names used, perhaps listed as advisers, and even refer to it on their own resumes without ever attending a meeting. (Others might be used without their permission. One survey asked schools to list the members of their vocational advisory committees. More than one-fifth of the "members" contacted had no knowledge of being on a committee [Massachusetts Dept. of Education 1986].)

The degree of effort one is willing to put into a volunteer project can vary dramatically, even day to day. An executive director whose program has several advisory boards and who herself sits on several more, points out that fluctuations of effort depend on priorities and other circumstances:

At first you are very enthusiastic about the committee. It's nice that you have been invited and your expertise has been recognized. So a lot of people come to the first meeting. Then when you really start rolling up your sleeves and getting into work, people realize that it's not just sitting around giving advice. There is work in between, conferences to attend, material to read and write. And you start wondering, does my participation in these meetings justify this amount of time and work? In a relatively short time, you start making choices. You get the agenda mailed to you and you wonder whether it is worth it.

I believe in what they are doing [with this project], and I like the fact that they are really listening, using our advice to shape the project, so I continue going. But of the original 25 members, sometimes our meetings have only five people. *

The amount of sustained effort volunteers are willing to put into an advisory committee is clearly a necessary (if not sufficient) factor in having an effective, active advisory committee. If most or all the members have stopped attending meetings or working on the committee, the committee functions at less than the desired level. The degree of effort volunteers put in daily or weekly is closely tied to the volunteers' expectations of the organization and their perception of how they are being treated. One dedicated and hardworking advisory committee member, without being asked, for several years prepared a monthly report for the staff, which never failed to thank her and tell her how useful it was. But when the staff became too busy to thank her, she stopped preparing and sending the reports.†

Organizations can help bring out volunteers' highest degree of effort by the way they treat their volunteers. Administrators should know what they want of volunteers, communicate well, provide meaningful and challenging jobs, and give volunteers plenty of recognition (Gibson 1986, p. 64). A list of volunteers' expectations clusters into six general areas (see table 2) (Goodale 1981): How well staff and administration meet these expectations is a powerful determinant of the degree of effort volunteers will sustain.

Integrating Motivation, Commitment, And Degree of Effort

Volunteers are complex mixes of commitment, motivation, and degree of effort, and the combinations contribute to the different roles committee members play, the amount of work the committee gets done, how effective it might be, and the

---

*Teitel 1992, interview notes.
†Teitel 1992, interview notes.

TABLE 2

A VOLUNTEER'S EXPECTATIONS

Clear and Constant Communication
- As a volunteer, I expect constant communication. I don't want to be put in an embarrassing position because the executive director has not clued me in.

A Well-Defined Relationship with Staff
- I . . . expect clarity about what the staff's and [committee's] responsibilities are. They can overlap; this isn't a black and white area. There is a vast gray area, but there still has to be a framework in which we have expectations [of] each other.
- I expect to have a professional relationship with the staff. I respect what staff members can bring to their jobs, but I expect the staff to recognize me as a bona fide coworker who has a professional attitude toward my job.

Respect for Volunteers' Time
- I would not dream of conducting a [committee] meeting without having all resources marshaled ahead of time. The [committee] should know that the staff will supply those resources.
- I expect the staff to see that the time I have committed is used wisely. I'm not going to tolerate going to a . . . meeting that is filled with trivia, where we don't make decisions or discuss meaty issues.

The Staff's Willingness to Listen
- I . . . have something to contribute that I think is important not only to the [committee] but [also] to the staff. I can bring a perspective from the field to the staff, and I expect the staff to listen.

Support for Volunteers' Role
- I expect guidance in my job. I want to be pushed occasionally. . . . I expect a staff member to be sensitive to this [expectation], to know when to push and how far to push. It's all part of the support I expect.
- I want training in my job. . . . Over the years, I've found that training or orientation is often inadequate.

Personal Growth and Recognition
- . . . I expect to have an opportunity for growth. I can always learn.
- I want some recognition, too. Sometimes I need only a simple "thank you." It means a lot to me to have a staff member say "Thanks so much for doing that professional job, for running that meeting so well, for being in control." . . . I want some respect for the contribution I'm making.

Source: Goodale 1981, pp. 33–35.

TABLE 3

MATRIX OF COMMITMENT, MOTIVATION, AND DEGREE OF EFFORT

Commitment: Volunteer is committed to:
- Organization
- Clients
- Volunteerism
- Social vision

Motivation: Volunteer is motivated by:
- Psychological needs, including altruism and needs for power, affiliation, and achievement
- Opportunities to try new skills
- Personal or professional growth

Degree of Effort: Volunteer's effort ranges:
- From a high level, in which he or she seeks additional tasks
- To a low level, in which he or she seeks to minimize the work

What causes a person to volunteer is a complex mix of these factors. For example:

- A client-centered individual volunteers as an opportunity to try new skills and is willing to expend high levels of effort as long as she feels she is learning from the experience.
- An individual with a strong commitment to social justice volunteers in the hope of meeting his needs for power and influence but exerts only minimum effort because he feels the organization's staff does not respect his opinions.

Source: Ilsley 1990, p. 35; J. Keller 1983.

different loyalties that might exist. The matrix of possibilities is shown in table 3.

Because volunteers are complex individuals, staff members interested in motivating volunteers as much as possible need to understand that "There's no such thing as a typical volunteer. . . . People don't volunteer without expectations. . . . Volunteer programs should be coordinated with volunteers in mind[, which] means planning tasks based on the individual's needs, recruiting [volunteers] by appealing to needs, supervising in a way that allows needs to be met, and rewarding people with what's important to them" (Henderson 1981, p. 26). How well staff, committee chairs, and others accom-

lish these tasks helps influence one determinant of a committee's effectiveness: If volunteers need to be highly involved
or an effective advisory committee, then the staff's attitudes
nd behaviors are critical. Volunteers' level of effort changes
asily and is extremely responsive to how they feel they are
eing treated by staff.

The single most important motivator to a volunteer is a
ense of accomplishing meaningful work, and how institu-
ional representatives structure and recognize that work is key.
'or some volunteers, "meaningful work" can be support or
ervice activities like fund-raising, public relations, or orga-
nizing staff recognition parties. But for others, the meaningful
work is giving advice, which could lead to conflicts if admin-
strators are reluctant to receive such advice. The next section
discusses group dynamics, including the idiosyncratic needs
nd motivations of volunteers and disagreements they might
have with institutional representatives about the committee's
ourpose and direction.

THE IMPACT OF GROUP DYNAMICS

Advisory committees are small work groups, subject to the personalities, social group norms, and all the other vicissitudes of the group process. This section draws a few key ideas from the literature on group dynamics that contribute to the discussion of an advisory committee's effectiveness, identifying first 11 tasks that all groups must face and second predictable stages groups go through before they gain cohesiveness and become effective. The section also asks whether the group's strong cohesiveness and standards of high performance are desirable features in an advisory committee.

Tasks Facing Any Group

To be effective, any group needs to resolve certain basic questions about how and why it operates. Any group, no matter its purpose, faces 11 tasks (table 4) (Cohen et al. 1988). Those involved in planning or establishing an advisory committee should review the list and make some choices: How advisory committees go about addressing these basic tasks shapes their direction, tone, purpose, and, ultimately, their overall effectiveness.

TABLE 4

TASKS FACING ANY GROUP

1. Atmosphere and relationships
2. Members' participation
3. Understanding and accepting goals
4. Listening and sharing information
5. Handling disagreements and conflict
6. Making decisions
7. Evaluating members' performance
8. Expressing feelings
9. Division of labor
10. Leadership
11. Attention to process

Source: Cohen et al. 1988, p. 144.

Atmosphere and relationships

What kinds of relationships should exist in an advisory committee? How formal and businesslike should meetings be? What role, if any, should socializing and developing personal relationships play? The first meeting of one newly formed advisory committee, for example, was purely social, with members getting to know each another informally. Some members liked that approach, while others just as obviously wanted to get down to business.* Planners need to find the right balance, factoring in institutional or programmatic goals, the personal predilections of the people to be involved, and the needs of the committee to accomplish something. And that decision needs to be made early, as the tone generally is set at the first meeting and could be hard to change later.

Members' participation

Are expectations for participation the same for all members? Does participation necessarily mean coming to meetings regularly—or even at all? The dean of one business school has an advisory committee of 30, only ten to 15 of whom ever come to meetings. Some, however, are available for telephone consultations, and he values their input. But he also inherited the committee with about a dozen members whom he has never seen or heard from in two years.† Planners need to decide whether people who never come to meetings (but consult on the telephone) are considered members and at what point members should be dropped for nonparticipation.

Understanding and accepting goals

Many, and sometimes conflicting, views exist of what advisory committees should do. Planners need to be clear about understanding goals and expectations, sort out how much agreement is necessary for a smoothly functioning group, and determine who decides where the emphasis and direction should be.

Listening and sharing information

How much information about the program should members of an advisory committee have? The flow of information often becomes the key ingredient that affects what roles the committee can take (King 1960). Framers of an advisory committee need to think through the implications of the flow of information and decide whether all information should be funneled through the director or dean, or whether members should have independent contacts with faculty and staff.

---

*Teitel 1991, interview notes.
†Teitel 1991, interview notes.

Handling disagreements and conflict

One of the most common conflicts is when members, either collectively or as individuals, make suggestions that the dean or director or staff do not wish to implement. Planners need to sort out how these and other less predictable areas of conflict should be resolved.

Making decisions

By definition, advisory committees are not decision-making bodies, only offering advice to program or college leaders and staff. But *how* will that advice be offered? Planners should think through procedures: Will the director or dean poll each member and then make the decision, possibly with the help of his or her staff or faculty? Will the committee, under the leadership of the chair, come to a decision and then present a unified position? Three common processes can contribute to the dissatisfactions people often express about how group decisions are made: decision by lack of response (letting suggestions "plop" and be ignored), decision by authority rule (usually by the chair), or decision by minority (an individual who railroads a decision without allowing discussion) (Schein 1969). Planners would do well to think about how these decision-making processes would affect an advisory committee's functioning.

Three common processes can contribute to the dissatisfaction people often express about how group decisions are made.

Evaluating members' performance

Because advisory committees are voluntary organizations, formal evaluation is not very relevant, but informal evaluation, measuring contributions and commitment, is common. Planners should think about how subcommittee chairs will be chosen and about who will be asked to continue on the committee when his or her term is over.

Expressing feelings

Do members of the advisory committee express personal feelings, and, if so, do they concern only the task? Will they be talked about openly and directly? People entering new groups face four kinds of emotional issues, regardless of the task: identifying what their role will be in the group, wondering whether they will be able to influence others, wondering whether the group's goals will meet their needs, and wondering whether the group will accept them and like them (Schein 1969). Planners should think about whether the group will address these basic issues.

Division of labor

Whether involved primarily in advising, supporting, or both, active advisory committees have a great deal of work to perform. To assume a leadership position in a voluntary organization (unlike in paid employment) usually means accepting more time-consuming and tedious work without the perquisites, such as clerical help, that usually accompany paid employment (Pearce 1980). Planners should consider whether committee and subcommittee chairs will do the bulk of the work, how tasks are to be assigned, and whether members of this volunteer organization will select their own activities or have them assigned.

In addition to considering how tasks will be divided *among* members of the advisory committee, planners need to look at the division *between* the advisory committee and the paid professionals of the college or university—deans, directors, staff, or faculty. They need to determine who will do the work between meetings and how that work will be delegated.

Leadership

Most advisory committees have a chair. Those planning the committee should determine whether the chair is to be an outsider or a staff or faculty member or administrator from the institution, and whether he or she is to be elected by the committee or appointed by the institutional representatives. Will the chair be a genuine leader, or is it a ceremonial position, with the leadership of the advisory committee coming from the dean or the faculty? And who sets the agenda and defines the scope of work for the committee?

Attention to process

Do procedures exist for monitoring and improving the process of the advisory committee? An important measure of a group's effectiveness, particularly for a voluntary one like an advisory committee, is the satisfaction of its members and their willingness to sustain activity over time (Hackman and Walton 1986). Groups should take a few minutes at the end of each meeting or on some periodic basis to ask members how they feel about what is going on (Schein 1969). Planners need to incorporate some attention to process and self-evaluation in their operations.

With these 11 issues as a checklist, administrators, faculty, or staff setting up an advisory committee can plan for and pay attention to details of group process.

Stages of Group Formation

Groups go through several predictable stages on their way to becoming high-performance groups (Cohen et al. 1988; Johnson and Johnson 1975; Lacoursier 1980), identified in some of the literature as "forming, storming, norming, and performing" (Arbuckle and Murray 1989). While groups predictably evolve through these stages, each stage could last for one hour or one year, and it is not possible to know ahead of time how long a particular stage will last (pp. 4–9). The process is not always smoothly linear, and groups might regress to an earlier stage with the addition of new members or a turnover of staff or when they face a particularly controversial issue. Nonetheless, the stages provide a useful framework for looking at the development of advisory committees and offer particular insights into those that never reach "performing" (table 5).

In general, relatively few groups reach the highly collaborative "performing" stage (Cohen et al. 1988), and those that are successful develop sufficiently strong connections, clear expectations, and effective processes in their forming and norming stages that allow them to survive the challenges and frustrations of the storming period. Many groups fail to do so and either fall apart or find their long-term effectiveness undermined by unresolved conflicts.

This framework of forming, storming, norming, and performing can be very useful for those thinking about and involved with advisory committees. For advisory groups, the challenge of reaching the high-performance stage is compounded by several factors. Generally, work teams and other groups are comprised of members from within an organization, but members of advisory committees come from outside, usually with relatively little knowledge of each other or about the institution. In the forming stage, this condition adds tasks, and committee members, often sorting out what it will be like to be associated with a new organization, usually have only a vague sense of what a committee or a committee member is supposed to do. In the formation of newer advisory committees, institutional representatives might themselves not be very clear about the focus, direction, and specific tasks of an advisory committee, so they are unable to provide the needed clarity and direction (Cochran, Phelps, and Cochran 1980). This lack of understanding and clarity could lead to dysfunctional advisory boards or to boards that form in

TABLE 5

TEAM DEVELOPMENT PROCESS

- **Forming:** Members are eager and have positive expectations. They are likely to wonder what the purpose of the group is, what their tasks will be, how the group will be led and organized, and how likely it is that their work will be fruitful. They depend on the leader.

- **Storming:** Members are dissatisfied and frustrated because their expectations and the reality of the team's work do not coincide. Dependence on the leader is not satisfying, appropriate resources are not readily available, and some problems are not easily solved. The frustration might lead to anger toward the leader or other members of the group, and could raise questions about the task and the goals.

- **Norming:** Members work toward resolution of the conflicts; personal satisfaction and self-esteem are heightened as expectations and reality are more clearly meshed and the group begins to figure out how to work together effectively. Beginning efforts at collaboration are reinforced by some early successes and positive feedback.

- **Performing:** Members are once again eager to be part of a team. They feel greater autonomy as well as a strong sense of mutual interdependence. Leadership functions are shared, and energy and time are focused on achieving the committee's purpose.

Source: Arbuckle and Murray 1989; pp. 4-7–4-9.

name only but remain paper committees (Gross 1980).

The storming stage can also be a difficult stage for advisory committees to survive. Members from outside an institution with relatively weak ties to it are less likely (than, say, employees) to stick through the frustrations of the storming period. They are, after all, volunteers; they can, and do, simply not reappear for subsequent meetings. And if the committee is still run by the director or dean or faculty, the dissatisfaction with the leader that commonly occurs during this phase could be directed against the institutional representative and lead to the committee member's withdrawal. This situation can easily be exacerbated by any differences about the kind of input expected, where members brought on for their expertise find they are expected to be rubber stamps (Light 1982).

Frequently groups pull through the storming stage by successfully completing some task together (Arbuckle and Murray 1989). Those who work with volunteer groups should give the groups an attainable task that will be visible and can contribute to the volunteers' continued belief that they are helping (O'Connell 1985). Especially in the start-up stage, volunteers should be given tasks that are doable in a short time and have visible results, even if the early activities are not crucial to the overall program (Blake, Beach, and Hopkins 1976). In terms of group dynamics, the successful completion of the task eases the group out of the storming stage and at the same time helps it define what its norms for operation are. This strategy can be risky for advisory committees, however, because of potential disagreements about the scope of the committee's input to the organization. A sense that a project is busy work can quickly undermine any developing group spirit and serve as a powerful demotivator (Wilson 1981).

Those advisory committees that reach the performing stage are characterized by a clear purpose and by collaborative roles. Before a group can reach high performance, it has to have a clear focus on whether it is to provide advice, support, or both. In a high-performance group, the meshing and sharing between the committee members and the staff or administration transcend the status of insider or outsider and exude a strong sense of people's working together for a common goal.

How Important Are the Group's Cohesion And High-Performance Norms?

The preceding discussion of high-performance norms and the group's cohesion assumes they are desirable features in an advisory committees. Yet advisory committees come in many different forms, with many different expectations for their involvement. The importance of these factors varies according to the committee's focus and differs depending on the amount of service or advice expected of it.

For an advisory committee's support or service roles, the group's unity and expectations of high performance are helpful but not necessary. An advisory group that rarely, if ever, meets and is not unified can still help the institution through the individual services of its members. In this sense, the group becomes a volunteer service organization. While it is important to recognize, to reward, and to respond to individual needs, it is not necessary for such a group to meet. On the other hand, successful meetings and a group that develops a sense of purpose, mission, and camaraderie will be more productive in supporting the institution. Members will be more likely to have a sense of ownership along with their involvement. With an advisory committee that provides service, the total output from a high-performing group will be much higher than the sum of individuals' output. A positive group spirit can dramatically increase the effectiveness of the group's service but is not essential to it.

For a committee's advisory role, the answer is more complex, and it depends more on exactly what type of advice is desired. Advice can be provided by individuals, making group dynamics irrelevant. In fact, it might be simpler for a dean or director to poll committee members on particular questions or consult with them on their areas of expertise. For this type of input, an active, cohesive advisory committee is neither necessary nor, possibly, desirable. As discussed earlier, getting input from an advisory committee can complicate a manager's life. Getting advice from individuals is considerably more flexible and leaves control in the hands of the director or staff, albeit at the expense of diverse or independent input. In a loosely knit council of advisers, however, a strong sense of ownership and involvement with a program or institution is less likely.

Many deans, directors, faculty, and staff consider the development of a strong sense of group unity a mixed blessing. While it brings the advantages of substantial, thoughtful input as the group develops a strong sense of ownership and involvement with the program or institution, it also has some risks. The committee might get too strong or too independent and might begin to overfunction, moving into areas outside its scope or mandate from institutional representatives.

In most cases, the representatives of the college or university who establish an advisory committee start the process with a great deal of power and influence over the direction and focus of the committee. They establish committees, convening them and determining their initial composition, agenda, and group norms. A strong, cohesive group can help balance this influence by giving greater power to the members of the advisory committee than they would have as individuals. They can collectively ask for information and suggest approaches that no one member could.

If it is not a unified, independent group, an advisory committee is easily controlled by institutional representatives. But an advisory committee is, after all, not a decision-making body. Institutions set up advisory committees to help improve their programs, and who is better positioned to direct and focus them than the staff, faculty, or administrators? On the other hand, if institutional representatives do not highly value advice or are too concerned that their committees might become overinvolved, they might curtail opportunities for the group to work together and lose some of the benefits that an active, involved committee can provide. Furthermore, external funders who mandate advisory committees do so to have them play more the role of independent watchdog, ensuring programmatic accountability and responsiveness to the community and underserved populations (Ibrahim et al. 1987). The appropriate balance point varies from situation to situation, but it is useful to understand what variables affect an advisory group's independence. Can committee members develop a cohesive, independent group even if institutional representatives do not want one?

Proponents of activist, independent advisory committees believe that it is possible and desirable to do so and have tried to teach group process skills to advisory committee members (Biagi 1978; California State 1988). For example, one way to motivate committee members to play a more active role is to question their level of satisfaction:

- Do members accept imposed agendas, goals, programs, and tasks without participating in their development?
- Is the communication primarily one way; that is, does the director or chair do most of the talking?
- Is leadership for only a few people, and do the rest follow?
- Are decisions always made by a higher authority, with little or no involvement by the council members?
- Is the council evaluated only in relation to goals, with little attention to how group members feel toward each other?
- Are meetings stiff and formal, and do they often seem pointless and a waste of time?
- Do council members have little opportunity to express opinions, feelings, and reactions? (Sweningson 1984, p. 3).

A "yes" answer to any of these questions indicates a need to improve the committee (Sweningson 1984), perhaps through a minicourse on group dynamics to enable committee members to have more influence and control over the committee's direction. The California Department of Education, for example, publishes guidelines for citizen advisory committees, providing instructional advice on the group process to help empower members. The advice includes handouts on understanding and analyzing roles in a group and clear (state-mandated) guidelines for the roles and responsibilities of committees and their members. It also makes more explicit the responsibility advisory committee members have to understand enough about group dynamics to become an activist committee:

> *Will a [citizen advisory committee] be an effective means of parent involvement or just window dressing for the school district it supposedly advises? A significant share of the responsibility rests with the members themselves* (California State 1988, p. 15).

This approach presupposes an adversary relationship between committee and staff that, one hopes, does not exist in most advisory committees in higher education. Nonetheless, the questions posed are good ones, and the underlying issue of an advisory committee's independence is an important one. An understanding of the factors that influence independence is useful to anyone interested in working effectively with advisory committees.

Factors Contributing to an Independent Advisory Committee

For a committee to successfully provide independent advice when the staff and administrators do not seek it, the committee must replace the norms and expectations placed by the staff with different ones that have evolved through the group process. The process of norming, or establishing the formal and informal sets of rules that will govern the committee's functioning, does not always follow the planner's intentions. Some norms are explicit, spelled out by the person who convenes the group—in this case, usually the deans, directors, and staff of the institutions setting up the advisory committee. At the outset, they might select the members, organize a schedule of meetings, set the agenda for the first meeting, and perhaps spell out expectations for the committee. Once the committee begins to function as a group, however, things might not evolve as planned.

Inevitably, because people are social beings with needs greater and more complex than those of machines, a variety of behaviors and attitudes will begin to emerge and over time take on relatively stable patterns. . . . It is this emergent (informal) system [that] gives the group its particular identity, its view of who should do what, who should have influence, and how close members should feel. Even the actual leadership of a group may emerge as different [from] the designated leader (Cohen et al. 1988, pp. 79–80.

This emergent group dynamic could be one in which committees push for real advisory roles—but only if the committee develops a sense of unity. The advisory committee that refused to be dismissed provides a rare but dramatic example of emergent processes that can occur. It took a crisis for the committee to pull together: "The fact that our task force was nearly abolished seemed to help us form a group loyalty" (Dahl 1986, p. 4). The likelihood that this group unity and a sense of independence will develop is influenced by three sets of factors: *membership* of the group, the ways its *meetings* are organized and run, and the clarity and scope of its *mandate* (table 6).

Membership

Composition. For genuine input from outside the institution, an advisory committee has to be comprised largely of outsiders. (Internal advisory committees within a large institution require members from other subunits.) Yet one study of advisory committees shows that, even when the committee's guidelines regarding accreditation specifically excluded faculty members from being voting members, in all cases they served, and in one case, membership was *limited* to faculty (Gross 1980). Further, members of the committee need to be somewhat independent from the organization, as clients currently receiving services might not be sufficiently independent. Similarly, the practice in vocational education of using adjunct faculty as "outside industry representatives" on advisory committees could prevent a truly objective review

Members of the committee need to be somewhat independent from the organization.

TABLE 6

ORGANIZATIONAL FACTORS INFLUENCING THE DEVELOPMENT OF AN INDEPENDENT ADVISORY COMMITTEE

A cohesive group dynamic, which can lead to an independent advisory committee, is more likely if the characteristics in Column I are present and less likely if the characteristics of Column II are present.

	I Increases Likelihood of Independent Committee	II Decreases Likelihood of Independent Committee
Membership		
Composition	Independent outsiders	Insiders (faculty or staff) or dependent outsiders
Selection of new members	Multiyear, revolving terms; selection is open and collaborative	Vague terms at the discretion of director; selection by director
Socialization of new members	By committee	By director or dean
Meetings		
Frequency and timing	Regular and frequent	Occasional, sporadic
Decision-making structure	Done as a group in regular meetings	Individuals polled by director
Control of agenda	Members (or outside chair) have input	Director or staff control
Leadership	Chaired by outsider, who takes real leadership	Chaired by director or staff member, or by outside figurehead
Mandate		
Charter	Clear, preferably written, expectations	Vague, subject to interpretation by director or staff
Access to information	Independent and comprehensive	Funneled through director or staff
Response to advice	Formal response to formal recommendations	No clear process or required response

of programs. In one community college where the president and dean tried to get vocational programs to be more responsive to industry, the administration spoke disparaging of advisory committees as "cozy clubs where adjunct faculty sit around and drink coffee" (Teitel 1991, p. 10).

Selection of new members. If members are appointed solely at the discretion of the institutional representatives (the most common pattern in the literature), the likelihood of the committee's developing independence is reduced. It is further reduced if the appointments are for short periods or if members serve at the discretion of the director. But committees with multiyear, revolving terms (so that only one-half or one-third of the members are replaced each year) that have a voice in selecting other members are more likely to develop and sustain a unity that will allow them to be independent.

Socialization of new members. If committee members can establish the norms for the group and socialize new members into them, the possibilities for independence are enhanced. New members can be socialized through a buddy system, where a new member is paired with a continuing one, through a handbook, or through a formal orientation. Again, the chances for an independent advisory committee increase if members are involved in the socialization process.

Meetings
Frequency and timing. Advisory committees that meet, say, only once or twice a year are also less likely to develop and mature as groups. Meetings held during working hours, at the convenience of the institutional staff (Baker and Ostertag 1981), could serve as a disincentive for members to attend and convey a message of their relative lack of importance, depending on the composition of the membership.

Decision-making structure. In some advisory committees, emergent group dynamics are curtailed because the committees operate less as a group than as a collection of individuals, with the dean or director at the hub. The informal use of the telephone to solicit quick advice from individual members can undercut the rest of the committee's involvement (Light 1982) and keep the committee from jelling as a group.

Control of agenda. One study shows that about 70 percent of the advisory committees surveyed had their agendas prepared by institutional representatives, with fewer than 20 percent involving committee members themselves (Baker and Ostertag 1981, p. 4). Another reports how common it is for staff to "stack the deck with agenda items and information" to make sure that problems they do not "want to deal with are left off the agenda" (Light 1982, p. 9). Not surprisingly, a majority of the committee members in Baker and Ostertag's study wanted the committee to be allowed to discuss new items that were not on the agenda (1981, p. 5). In addition to being able to influence the agenda, opportunities for committee members to talk without staff present can contribute to a more independent advisory committee.

Leadership. For a committee to develop any unity and independence, the chair must be from outside the institution and must truly chair the committee, not just serve as a figurehead. Yet in one study, almost two-thirds of advisory committee chairs are the self-appointed institutional representatives, with most of the relatively few outsiders who serve as chairs appointed by the institution (Baker and Ostertag 1981, p. 3). Even when regulations forbid school employees from serving on advisory committees (let alone chairing them), more than half of the survey respondents reported that a school representative chairs their committee (Massachusetts Dept. of Education 1986, p. 6).

Mandate
Charter. Committees with clear charters given them by the program or institution can develop greater autonomy, because their activities are less subject to the staff's or administration's discretion. Further, members can interpret written charters directly, without their being filtered through the eyes of the institutional staff. Handbooks and other formal documents can give members the information and authority they could need to exercise some independence.

Access to information. How much information advisory committee members get, and who controls its flow, are keys that affect what roles the committee can take (King 1960).

Lacking information, or having only that [the] program staff members may be willing to share, or [having infor-

*mation that] can be gleaned [only] from random contact
with program clients, advisory groups will be unlikely to
acquire the basis of knowledge necessary to support a meaningful advisory role. The result may be a sense of impatience
and frustration among advisory group members* (Miller
1987, p. 282).

How much access to information an institution is willing to
provide its committee is a critical choice that determines the
level and scope of the committee's functioning (Laney 1984).

Response to advice. Another important part of the mandate
for an advisory committee is the process of responding to its
advice. If committees function as groups (not as individual
advisers surrounding a director), they will recommend courses
of action occasionally. What happens to those recommendations is key. If the committee is being taken seriously as a
source of input, its formal recommendations should trigger
formal responses, including an explanation of why any recommendations are rejected (Light 1982, p. 38).

The process of group dynamics underscores variables relat-
ing to membership, meetings, and the committee's mandate
that will determine whether a committee is likely to develop
an independent, unified spirit. The next section uses a case
study to look at these issues in more depth.

HOW INDEPENDENT CAN AN ADVISORY COMMITTEE GET? A Case Study

This section discusses an example of an advisory committee that tried to establish its own independence, showing how committee members, especially if they come with a predetermined agenda, can steer an advisory committee toward greater autonomy and more of an advisory role than the director and staff desired. It concludes with an analysis that integrates the factors—expectations, motivation, and group dynamics—discussed in the preceding three sections.

The Case

The committee was a mandated one. A directive from the chief academic officer required all institutes and centers of the university to have an internal "faculty advisory council" comprised of faculty from other units within the university. This ongoing group would be in addition to a periodic review conducted by an outside team every few years. The center's director requested nominations from various deans and established a committee of ten members, who were invited for a luncheon and opening meeting in late November.

At the first meeting, the director and two top staff people spoke for the first hour, describing the center and its mission and funding and explaining the committee's role: to serve as a two-way pipeline to the rest of the campus.

DIRECTOR: We want you to let people on campus know who we are and what we are doing. We want to involve faculty more in what we do. We see you as a breath of fresh air. You can ask us questions, maybe get involved in some consulting with us. . . . We don't anticipate this to be a do-nothing committee. [He went on to describe the center's finances and several projects that faculty might get involved in. Near the end of the first hour, he said,] If this is really to be two way, I should shut up.

MEMBER #1: What processes do you have in place for faculty members to get involved with the center? To whom does someone apply?

DIRECTOR: There is no real process. If we had a process, we would have to announce it, and it would get very formal. We don't like to operate that way. Come and see us. We'll have a meeting like this one. That's the way we're operating. We want you to tell them about it.

MEMBER #2: You might see us, as the advisory committee, as a way to suggest a process, but you don't seem to really want to have one. It makes me wonder how much input you really want.

DIRECTOR: [Starts to respond but is cut off]

MEMBER #3: Let me speak before you. [The director] has said that he wanted the advisory committee to be more than just a pipeline. He wants us to advise as much as possible, to be a pipeline for communication, and to raise questions. Fine. I think the next step is for us ten members to meet by ourselves and to talk about how we wish to govern ourselves.

ASSISTANT DIRECTOR: I strongly endorse another meeting with the center's staff. If the advisory committee wants to meet by itself, [hesitates] that's fine, but why?

MEMBER #3: Advisory committees always meet separately, to set up self-governance. If the committee is going to be objective, it needs to do that.

MEMBER #2: Yes, we need to get our own group dynamic going—together.

ASSISTANT DIRECTOR: Well, I've been on other advisory committees, and we never met separately.

DIRECTOR: Let's not spend a lot of time talking about the process; let's just do it. You can have your meeting, but there will be no lunch. [laughter]

MEMBER #3: The committee will meet by itself for the first hour. After we have done that, we will meet with the center's staff to get a notion of what the center wants.

DIRECTOR: I can tell you right now what we want. The key issue is that there is little communication with the rest of the campus. We need help telling others what we are doing and responding to their concerns. As for our own processes: We run the center and the processes are internal to us. We don't need any help with them.

The next meeting was held a week later. For the first hour, the committee met without any staff from the center and discussed two sets of processes. One was about the center and its internal policies: how the staff decided to hire people, what criteria they used for awarding grants, and, in general, how they made their decisions. To learn more about these matters, committee members developed a list of information and internal documents on guidelines and procedures to request of the director. The other process discussed was how the committee was to relate to the staff. Members looked at the language of the mandate from the university that had established the committee in the first place. "Are we just a sounding board of individuals, which is what the director seems to want, or are we a real advisory committee, which is what the university's guidelines seem to imply?" asked one member. The committee decided to use the university's definition as a mandate and to push for access to the kind of information it would need to do so effectively. After an hour, the director knocked on the door and was told to wait in the hall. After a brief delay, he was invited in, followed by the entire senior staff, looking very somber.

DIRECTOR [tight-lipped]: What's up?

MEMBER #3: We've been meeting to talk about the definition of our role. We see from the university's guidelines that ours is to be a "regular, long-term" involvement with the center. It seems we are not to be involved in personnel matters, but we have been trying to clarify what kinds of things we can provide advice on. We also wanted to make explicit the kinds of information we will need to do our job. We will need a list of all personnel, the center's command structure, how responsibilities are allocated, how fellows are appointed, and what the philosophy of the center's publication is.

MEMBER #4: These requests go beyond our individual interest. We feel strongly that if we are to be a valuable long-term asset, we need information about the underlying structure.

DIRECTOR: [After summarizing items requested to make sure he understood all of them and ticking off how and when he would provide each item,] Everything you said I agree with. There is nothing I am trying to hide.

Shortly after the meeting, committee members were given the materials they had requested. In some cases, existing documents were simply made available to members; in others, documents had to be developed in response to the inquiry.

After this brief flurry of activity, winter vacation came. Committee members talked about getting together soon, even if not convened by the center's staff, but did not follow through. The staff called only one more committee meeting, in midspring. At the start of the next academic year, all the members were thanked for their service and were told that, in the interests of involving other faculty members, the entire committee was being replaced.

The Issues

This case highlights several issues that frequently emerge in advisory committees, especially for mandated boards. The center's staff and some of the committee members had very different expectations about the range and focus of the committee's activities. With different ideas about how much advice the committee was to give, the battle was fought at committee meetings—over how much information the members could get, whether it could run itself and set its own agenda, and whether it could meet without staff.

The attitudes and expectations of administration and staff

The staff and director of the center did not ask to form an advisory committee: It was forced on them. They were quite comfortable with the close-knit, informal, and unpublicized decision-making process they had used since the center was founded ten years earlier. When establishing a faculty advisory committee was mandated, staff made the best of it by seeing it as a way to increase ties with faculty from around the university. They were not, however, interested in modifying, or even making public, any of the center's internal processes, and they were caught off guard by the request to hold the next meeting without them. The request came within the first few minutes of open discussion and came from two members who quickly moved to back each other up. (One of them even cut off the director to speak in support of his colleague.) The fact that they supported each other and confidently and matter of factly talked about advisory committees "always meeting separately" and the need for "self-governance" gave them considerable power in group dynamics. Even though the other members of the newly forming committee were just as taken by surprise as the staff was by the notion of meeting separately, the concerted action of two members forced the director's hand. To not agree made him look as though he were trying to cover something up or to prevent the committee's developing its proper function.

By agreeing to the separate meeting, however, he gave up a measure of control, something he was visibly aware of. The highly symbolic moment when the director was told to wait in the hall while the committee finished its private meeting underscores this loss, and the demand for information that hitherto had not been available is a substantive indication of that loss of control. The director acceded to each demand but regained overall control by calling only one more meeting and then dismissing the entire committee.

The motivation and commitment of committee members

Two of the members (#2 and #3 in the case study) came to the committee with an underlying commitment to try to open the center to public scrutiny, feeling that too many decisions were made behind closed doors. They had planned the coup that established an independent session for the committee. Thus, when one spoke up, the other was ready to cut off the director and support his colleague. With determination and mutual support, they were able to gain several allies, some of whom acknowledged that they would not have been so assertive by themselves but were happy to see the center's processes opened up. Their strategy had some limited success: Although the staff started without any apparent intent to share or make public the center's internal policies and procedures, the independent committee forced them to do so. Once the motivating factor of opening up the center's policies was partially met, their amount of effort dropped off. When the staff waited for several months before calling another meeting, some of the ardor ebbed from the volunteer committee members. Although they had talked of calling a meeting even if the staff did not, no one followed up on the suggestion. And after another four months without any meetings, when the entire committee was dismissed, no one protested. The center had a chance to start fresh with a presumably less independent advisory committee.

Thus, when one spoke up, the other was ready to cut off the director and support his colleague.

The impact of group dynamics

Several key elements made it possible for this advisory committee to have some influence, even though the center's staff did not welcome it.

- The coalition formed by two members was very effective in shaping the direction of a new group, especially in its early stages.

- The strategy of meeting apart was critical in allowing the group a chance to develop its own norms and establish its own goals out of the staff's and director's sight and control. Even an hour was an important step, and telling the director to wait in the hall symbolically helped cement the independence the committee was developing.
- The existence of an outside mandate (from the university) that created the advisory committee was important. The fact that the mandate was in writing allowed committee members to see the document and interpret it directly (not through the filters of the center's staff).
- The demand for information was a key first step toward having any input. By establishing what types of information it needed (as opposed to what the staff wanted to share), the committee took a major step toward potential input and, in doing so, accomplished one of the aims of the key movers on the committee.

Three key factors mitigated against the committee's continuing input:

- The *volunteer* status of the committee, coupled with the partial success in reaching the goals of opening up the center's processes, led to diminishing effort as members let other priorities in their lives come ahead of this one.
- The independence the committee established for itself never went so far as to include its calling a meeting. When it was left to the center's staff to call the next meeting, a long time elapsed, further cooling members' ardor.
- Finally, and of greatest long-term significance, the committee never established control of its successorship. The mandate from the university was silent about length of term (although most ongoing committees usually change only one-half or one-third of their membership each year to allow for continuity). With no clear policy or precedent, the control of successorship was left in the hands of the center, which used it to start with a fresh committee.

An understanding of the goals of institutional representatives, the commitment and motivation of committee members, and the processes of group dynamics can provide important insights into how the direction and effectiveness of advisory committees are shaped.

SUGGESTIONS FOR STARTING AND SUSTAINING AN ADVISORY COMMITTEE

This section focuses on practical suggestions for setting up and sustaining effective advisory committees. The most explicit literature on how to set up and manage effective advisory committees is targeted toward educators involved in vocational education in secondary schools or community colleges. As noted earlier, federal legislation in the last two decades has increased the role to be played by advisory committees in vocational education, and many specific instructional manuals are targeted at teachers and school and college administrators (see, e.g., Cochran, Phelps, and Cochran 1980; King 1960; Maryland State Advisory Council 1984; Office of the State Director 1987; Ohio State University 1985; Riendeau 1977).

In contrast, advice on how to set up and maintain advisory committees for other programs and in other types of institutions of higher education is much scarcer. In fact, when the president of Emory University urged his colleagues in *AGB Reports* to make better use of advisory committees, he based his how-to section on a handbook produced by the Indiana State Advisory Council on Vocational Education (Laney 1984). For this section, advice about vocational education advisory committees is augmented, when appropriate, by suggestions on advisory committees from other sectors of higher education (Brawer and Gates 1981; Doti 1989) or the nonprofit sector (Axelrod 1991), as well as from applicable aspects of the literature on governing boards (Houle 1990; O'Connell 1985).

The suggestions are organized around four aspects of the process of establishing and maintaining advisory committees: planning and establishing advisory committees, orienting members and conducting meetings, developing an organizational structure and scope for the committee's involvement, and rewarding and evaluating committees.

Planning and Establishing an Advisory Committee
Preliminary work
Before setting up an advisory committee, educators should clarify the committee's purpose and function and establish clearly how its work will dovetail with existing structures of organizational decision making. Background work should include understanding the history of and any previous roles played by advisory committees in the school or college. Organizers should write a brief statement clarifying the com-

mittee's purpose, responsibility, structure, and role and seeking internal approval, with a time line for implementation that would include securing teachers' and administrators' acceptance (Cochran, Phelps, and Cochran 1980, pp. 224–29).

Size

The committee's size should be determined by balancing the trade-offs between increased representation and the greater unwieldiness inherent in large committees. In general, committees with 20 or more members are more appropriate for institutionwide efforts and can involve greater representation from the community. On the other hand, they are likely to meet less frequently than committees of five to 12 members, which might be more suitable for a specific program area (Riendeau 1977). A larger committee has some inherent risks:

An advisory committee of 30 to 40 members cannot meet frequently, [which] limits its usefulness, and much of the business is consequently handled by subcommittees, while the advisory committee itself takes on the nature of an annual conference. In such circumstances, there is a risk that keen committee members who are not on the subcommittee will lose interest (King 1960, p. 25).

Selection

Exactly which segments of a community should be represented on the committee depends on the program or institution. For instance, vocational education programs might be particularly sensitive to the inclusion of union representatives (Corley 1988), but such an issue is less important in many university advisory committees. What is important is that the various aspects of the field or discipline the program is connected to are represented. Those oriented toward practice in a field must be balanced with those whose focus is research. Types and sizes of industries could be important, as illustrated by the experience of an advisory committee for a hotel/restaurant program at a community college:

One of the problems with the advisory committee as it was structured was that it represented only a segment of the industry (mom-and-pop motels) and not the big motel/hotel chains. One of the major restructurings of the program that eventually took place was the inclusion of the major hotel

*chains in the program, for the program was not meeting
the needs of those chains.**

For programs or disciplines, function and focus are important determinants of the composition of an advisory committee. For an institution, a widely inclusive approach might be suitable, modified as appropriate:

*Each community and region has its power structure, its
union and civic leaders, and care must be exercised in the
selection of committee members so that they are truly a
cross-section of the community or region to achieve balance.
Not only should representation of community or regional
leaders, minority group leaders, educational leaders, other
institutions, civic and other organizations, business and
industry be achieved in addition to geographical representation, but also the membership should represent various
business levels of administration—professional, technical,
skilled, semiskilled, presidents, vice presidents, and hourly
employees* (Oen 1985, p. 4).

Others advocate more focused committee membership, in some cases restricting membership to chief executive officers (Wilson 1981). Some suggest taking into account age, sex, residence, ethnic background, and type of job responsibilities by composing a grid that lists existing and potential board members by those criteria (Houle 1990). Sometimes members are targeted for specific items or talents they can offer: for example, a list that includes each member, his or her attendance, special activities (committee chair, speaker), and amount of money donated (Doti 1989).

The personality characteristics of potential members are also a factor. Members should be competent in their fields and have the respect of the people they work with, they should have the interest and adequate time to be involved in the committee, they should be of "good character" (Riendeau 1977), and they should be enthusiastic and able to work well in groups (Corley 1988, p. 7). Problems can arise with boards made up of aggressive people with professional expertise if the abrasive ones are not tempered with "a good sprin-

---

*Comments from an anonymous reviewer.

kling of equally bright people who also [have] the qualities of judgment, patience, fairness, and conciliation" (O'Connell 1985, p. 63).

To find members who meet these criteria, educators are urged to consult community leaders, religious leaders, and heads of volunteer organizations or appropriate professional organizations (O'Connell 1985). When members represent specific organizations, that organization should be asked to make the selection (King 1960), although individuals elected by their organizations might be less committed and motivated to be active members.

Once a few members have been invited to join the committee and have accepted their role on it, they could be asked to nominate others, not only simplifying a "sometimes difficult and time-consuming task," but also "ensur[ing] good working relationships within the committee" (Riendeau 1977, p. 11). Doing so, however, might work against the goals of diverse backgrounds and/or opinions. Instead, a broad and open nominating process that establishes a pool of perhaps 20 or 25 diverse potential members might be preferable (Light 1982). This pool could be winnowed to eight to ten, but not handpicked by one or two individuals. "Hand selection (selecting one's friends or think-alikes) would tend to restrict the input of the members, and the output of the committee would too often be a regurgitation of the ideas of the few persons selecting the committee" (p. 32). Others suggest seeking out potential opponents and using membership on the advisory committee as a way to co-opt them:

> *An advisory council provides a unique opportunity for derailing detractors of a program. If he or she doesn't like the direction that a training program is taking, the council provides that person a forum to air the grievance. If such a person declines to serve or offer assistance, he or she effectively abdicates the right to be critical in other settings* (Office of the State Director 1987).

Educators should not handpick members who will be favorable to the program or otherwise load the committee (Cochran, Phelps, and Cochran 1980). A balance is necessary to ensure a committee that represents diverse opinions, is not loaded with proponents or opponents, and still can function effectively.

Appointment

The request to become a member of an advisory committee should come from the highest possible authority to let potential members know the importance of their task (Corley 1988). Such an official invitation from the highest authority also helps clarify the chain of command and should make clear that the committee is to be advisory in nature (King 1960). For academic advisory committees, that person would be the college president or chief academic officer. The official request should come after a personal visit or telephone call to solicit interest in serving on the committee (Oen 1985).

A broad consensus exists in the literature that committee members should be asked to serve finite terms of about three years, with staggered replacement dates so the committee can serve with continuity as well as be renewed (Corley 1988; Houle 1990; Office of the State Director 1987). Members should not be reappointed after their terms expire, as automatic reappointment establishes a precedent and effectively means terms are indefinite (King 1960). This policy provides a simple way of removing unproductive members, while those whose services are particularly valuable can be reappointed after a year and tapped privately, or as a consultant, in the interim (p. 26). Members who do not attend a certain number of consecutive meetings could be automatically dropped (O'Connell 1985).

Orienting Members and Conducting Meetings
Orientation

Proper orientation is vital, and it should begin with the first contact that leads to the request to participate in the committee:

> *The orientation process for new members starts as the individuals are being selected and appointed to the committee. Much of [it] may occur in the process of convincing the individual of the importance of serving on the committee or when describing the program and the role of the advisory committee. Adequate attention, however, must be focused on this task because the haphazard orientation of new members can result in a committee that does nothing, or one that extends beyond its intended purpose* (Cochran, Phelps, and Cochran 1980, p. 237).

A handbook prepared by the educational institution is the best way to orient new members (see, e.g., Oen 1985, pp. 14–24), although fewer than half of the advisory committees in one survey had even so much as a written outline of their committees' responsibilities, let alone a handbook (Hartley 1980). If no handbook is available, each new member should be provided, individually or at the first meeting, with an overview of educational offerings and a discussion of specific career programs, an explanation of the role of the advisory committee, recent accomplishments of the advisory committee, the responsibilities and duties of members, a list of advisory committees and their members, an organizational structure, and a schedule of meetings (Cochran, Phelps, and Cochran 1980, pp. 237–38). A "host" or "buddy" could be assigned to each new member to assist in the orientation (O'Connell 1985), and committee members should have access to a library of written materials on their role and function (Corley 1988; Houle 1990). The committee chair, too, should receive in-service training (Corley 1988; Houle 1990).

Conducting meetings

The first meeting of the advisory committee is the most important, as it sets the tone for future meetings and helps establish relationships among committee members and between the committee and institutional representatives (King 1960). Unlike subsequent meetings, where staff will be present primarily to listen, the first meeting is usually chaired by the relevant faculty member or administrator (Cochran, Phelps, and Cochran 1980). (See Brawer and Gates 1981, pp. 20–21, Cochran, Phelps, and Cochran 1980, pp. 238–41, and Office of the State Director 1987, p. 9, for sample agendas for first and subsequent meetings.)

An instructional module on maintaining an occupational advisory committee (Ohio State University 1985) outlines a strategy for the first three meetings that orients new members and provides a transition to committee members' running the committee. The strategy starts with an educator-convened and -run first meeting, where school personnel plan everything, down to the placement of ashtrays (if smoking is permitted). During the first meeting, subcommittees should be set up to develop rules and bylaws for the advisory committee and an annual plan of work. At the second meeting, in addition to discussing the rules and annual work plan, the group should discuss one particular programmatic focus of concern. By the end of the third meeting, the rules and annual plan should have been accepted, officers have been elected in accordance with the rules, and the committee have had some experience working together on a focused issue. At that point, the educator's role should be phased out of active leadership to become more of a consultant or facilitator (Ohio State University 1985, pp. 10–15).

In general, the tone of meetings should be informal but businesslike (Oen 1985). Overly formal proceedings could reduce, not increase, the amount of advice offered by a committee. Refreshments should be served, and valuable socializing (and team building) can be expected to take place during breaks (Ohio State University 1985). Meetings should not exceed two hours during the day, three hours during the evening, and five hours for an all-day session (King 1960).

The literature suggests a range for the optimum number of times to meet—a minimum of four meetings per year and special meetings only as needed, because "council members are busy people and assisting the educational community without compensation is probably not one of their highest priorities" (Office of the State Director 1987, p. 13); or monthly meetings, with a requirement that at least six meetings be held per year (Maryland State Advisory Council 1984); or at least one meeting a year (Corley 1988); or one meeting near the start of school, one near the end, and as many in between as the committee agrees to (Riendeau 1977). New committees might wish to meet more frequently for the first few years.

Each member should have minutes of meetings to track what has happened and to keep a record for committee members to look back on their accomplishments (Cochran, Phelps, and Cochran 1980).

Developing an Organizational Structure and Scope
Organizational structure
A typical advisory committee is organized around a chair, a vice chair, and a secretary. Because the position of secretary often requires a significant amount of work between meetings, the secretary should be a representative of the institution (Cochran, Phelps, and Cochran 1980). But doing so can also have the (possibly unintended) effect of making it easier for institutional representatives to manipulate the committee, for it gives them "control of the minutes," allowing them to avoid

Overly formal proceedings could reduce, not increase, the amount of advice offered by a committee.

recording certain things that were said and to highlight others.* Many authors suggest that the chair be a member of the community, elected by the committee (Baker and Ostertag 1981; King 1960; Light 1982). It is vital that institutional administrators see the chair as the head of the committee; otherwise, "the hard-to-define and difficult-to-establish successful working relationships within a committee can be shattered by the feeling that the [chair] is only a figurehead" (Cochran, Phelps, and Cochran 1980, p. 247).

Once the committee has started functioning, the institutional representative's role in running it should drop to one of facilitator or consultant. Key staff should work with the chair to establish the agenda, although the chair bears ultimate responsibility for determining the agenda (Cochran, Phelps, and Cochran 1980; Ohio State University 1985).

Most of the instructional literature encourages clear delineation of the roles and responsibilities of the advisory committee and its members in bylaws and a constitution (Cochran, Phelps, and Cochran 1980; Maryland State Advisory Council 1984). While a formal set of bylaws does help clarify roles and responsibilities, the structure should not be made overly formal, setting up a "rigid set of rules that [might] destroy the initiative of members of the committee and impede the fulfillment of its objectives" (King 1960, p. 33).

Scope of the committee's involvement

Perhaps one of the hardest tasks for an advisory committee is to clarify the scope of activities expected of it. Without proper orientation, an advisory committee could turn into one that "does nothing, or one that extends beyond its intended purpose" (Cochran, Phelps, and Cochran 1980, p. 237). It is important that committee members feel their efforts have a "discernible and meaningful purpose" (Office of the State Director 1987, p. 13). While committee members do not want to be used as rubber stamps, "usually reflected later in poor attendance and resignations" (Riendeau 1977, p. 23), they should not get too involved in day-to-day or administrative details (Corley 1988; Oen 1985; Office of the State Director 1987). A step toward resolving the dilemma entails making a detailed work plan outlining the issues the commit-

---

*Comments from an anonymous reviewer.

:ee will address in the year to come (Ohio State University 1985). The development and implementation of these work plans take on a cyclical process as the committee evolves:

> *The committee would normally start by developing an* awareness *of the existing programs or committee purpose,* move to an identification *of goals or problems, complete an* assessment *of needs and directions, identify and establish* priorities, *develop plans or strategies for a* program of work, *express concerns or recommendations in a* report, *and then start a new cycle* (Cochran, Phelps, and Cochran 1980, p. 278, emphasis in the original).

This cycle provides an opportunity, in advance, to clarify the scope of the committee and offers a framework for the committee to review what it has done.

Some activities "lend themselves more readily than others" to a committee's involvement: for example, technical assistance when solutions are sought and committee members have expertise; and specific, short-term assignments that lead to a "concrete or observable result," such as a public relations campaign or program evaluation (King 1960). A committee is less effective when approval, rather than advice, is sought (for example, the committee is being used as a rubber stamp for a decision that has already been made); when the speed of a response is critical and the advice sought will require considerable preparation by committee members; when committee members are likely to disagree strongly in their deliberations; or when administrative matters are being discussed (p. 40).

It is important to decide who has the expertise:

> *The key to asking for help is that the teacher must be willing to accept advice. In a like manner, if the instructor is more knowledgeable in an area than committee members, such as how to teach the course, then he or she should not direct them to provide input in that area* (Corley 1988, p. 10).

Regardless of the advisory committee's agreed-upon scope, input from the committee must be clearly directed through appropriate channels so as to respect the chain of command and to avoid bypassing any portion of the administrative hierarchy (Cochran, Phelps, and Cochran 1980).

Rewarding and Evaluating Committees
Recognizing advisory committee members
Although probably the best reward for a committee member
is to see the committee's suggestions implemented (King
1960), most of the instructional literature spells out a variety
of ways for institutions to show appreciation: plaques presented to members at the end of their service, special presentations at the committee member's last meeting, special luncheon ceremonies, or acknowledgment in the institution's
newsletter (Axelrod 1991, pp. 14–15). Ongoing acknowledgment of committee members during their term of service is
important, perhaps through dinners and cookouts, letters of
appreciation to members and their supervisors, invitations
to special events or special privileges (like parking or passes
to athletic events), and mention of names and activities in
handbooks, publications, bulletin boards, and news releases
(Cochran, Phelps, and Cochran 1980, pp. 272–73).

Evaluating the committee
While advisory committees are sometimes used to evaluate
programs, they are rarely subject to evaluation themselves;
such an evaluation, however, should be planned at the establishment of the committee (Cochran, Phelps, and Cochran
1980). Having the committee evaluate itself gives it some practice at what could be one of its most important functions. At
the same time, it shows others in the organization that the
committee's commitment to evaluation does not extend just
to judging others, but that it is willing to look critically at its
own practices. Alternately, committees could be evaluated
by members of the community, with such evaluations focused
on how representative the committee is and whether it has
open lines of communication and connects well with important segments of the population (Cochran, Phelps, and Cochran 1980; Riendeau 1977). The committee and affiliated staff
of the institution can also jointly evaluate the committee's work.

The workings of the group should be continuously evaluated (Brawer and Gates 1981). At the end of each meeting,
the chair, secretary, and college representative should meet
to review key features of the meeting and ask the following
questions:

- Was the agenda appropriate?
- Was the meeting conducted satisfactorily?

- What were the principal outcomes?
- Did the items on the agenda evoke interest and discussion by the committee? Did all members understand them? Were they valid, within the committee's field of interest, and important?
- Was the back-up material sent out in time and in the proper form?
- Was the meeting room adequate for the meeting?
- Who is acting on suggestions made at the meeting? Will the minutes be ready to be mailed in a reasonable amount of time? Have all items requiring special attention been identified? Who is handling them? Is the college prepared to keep commitments made to the committee members? Do special tasks, reports, or assignments call for immediate attention?
- Was the committee qualified to address the questions brought before it? Did the committee understand the underlying problems before rendering advice or suggesting a solution?
- Based on the way the committee handled this problem, what other problems should be directed to it? Should the problems have been handled by an advisory committee or another college group? (Brawer and Gates 1981, pp. 18–19).

—oOo—

Although the sources summarized in this section provide a great deal of useful nuts-and-bolts information, they are presented with a word of caution. Most of these works make two key assumptions. First, they are written with one perspective in mind—that of deans, directors, and institutional staff members. Second, they assume that these institutional representatives really want a great deal of advice. The next section concludes this report by setting those assumptions aside. It looks at these issues from multiple perspectives, including those of advisory committee members and of external groups and individuals. It also raises the possibility that some institutional representatives and some committee members might prefer not to be involved with a committee that is really advisory.

CONCLUSION

Advisory committees help organizations by connecting them to their environments. They can provide service to an institution in the outside world by helping to raise funds, recruit personnel, promote public relations, and improve links with other organizations. Advisory committees can also bring advice from outsiders to improve management and to review and evaluate the institution's mission, programs, and services (Cuninggim 1985). When used for advice, advisory groups represent a powerful mechanism to help institutions of higher education respond to their changing environments. When used for service, they provide important institutional support as well as positive experiences for the volunteer committee members themselves.

Advisory committees provide various levels of input into programs and institutions. Some are primarily ceremonial, combining occasional dinner meetings with general information sharing about the program. Many exist solely on paper or rarely meet. Others serve as rubber stamps to ratify decisions that have already been made. These different levels of service can satisfy the different needs and desires of the staff and administrators setting up the committees, and they can also meet the needs of many members. But problems often arise over expectations of how much advice the committee will offer and how deans, directors, and staff will use it. Individuals who are asked to join an advisory committee because of their knowledge or expertise sometimes end up disillusioned or disappointed if they find that their input is not valued or wanted. On the other hand, program directors, deans, and faculty or staff involved with advisory committees often find that it takes a great deal of time and effort to work effectively with a committee and that the advice they get complicates their own decision making. Not every manager or staff member has the time and skills or is inclined to believe that the benefits of the committee's input justify the effort and complications it might bring.

Most of the literature about advisory committees is written for institutional staff or administrators, who are told what they "should" do to develop a high level of input and support from advisory groups. By focusing primarily on telling them how to run advisory committees, the instructional literature assumes that the use of the committee's advice will increase if the knowledge and skill of institutional representatives are increased.

This report takes a different approach, acknowledging that many directors and staff members—and many committee members—do not want a lot of advice or service from an advisory committee. It builds on the factors identified as determinants of an effective advisory committee (attitudes, motivation, and group dynamics) and argues that any suggestions for improving a committee's effectiveness must take into account institutional representatives' attitudes about receiving input; the complex interplay of commitment, motivation, and degree of effort of the volunteer committee members; and organizational variables that influence whether or not a group assumes a strong advisory role.

A more relativistic, but possibly more realistic, set of suggestions is presented for all the people who are involved in one way or another with advisory committees: deans, directors, faculty and staff members, committee members and officers, and other outsiders concerned with the effectiveness of advisory committees. The advice takes into account the different goals of each party and suggests ways for each to get the type of advisory committee he or she wants.

Practical Advice for Institutional Representatives
Clarifying goals

The first step for a dean, director, or staff or faculty member responsible for working with an advisory group is to clarify goals, both of committee members and of the organization. What is really wanted from an advisory committee? Does the program or department or college need external input to shape its programs? Will it in the near future? How much control should be retained in establishing the focus and topic of advice? How will advice from the committee affect administrators' management style? Is the committee existing or a new one? In either case, why does the committee exist? Is it mandated by the institution or some external party? Is the mandate monitored in some way?

How much and what kind of support do administrators want from the committee?

Administrators should sort out the kinds and levels of support or service they hope to get from the advisory committee. Are specific support activities or projects available for members, or will they identify their own? If the committee is expected

to provide a sustained high level of involvement, how will
volunteer committee members be recognized and rewarded?
Can the service be provided by individual committee members, or will it be more effective if the committee operates
as a cohesive group?

How much and what kind of advice do administrators want from the committee?

Where on the following continuum do administrators' wishes
fall? Do they want:

1. No advice or input, but possibly some support and service
   in the outside community?
2. No advice, but it is necessary to set up a committee to
   meet external requirements (although it will not be
   closely monitored)?
3. The appearance of advice, to defuse critics and/or to
   satisfy some external monitoring requirements for an advisory committee?
4. Advice on more peripheral matters, or a sounding board
   for new ideas and experimental approaches?
5. Actual substantive advice on issues and processes that are
   central to the institution, with the focus to be determined
   by administrators?
6. Actual substantive advice on whatever issues and processes
   the advisory committee members think will improve the
   institution or program?

Perhaps what administrators really want is not advice, but
the other services and functions an advisory committee can
offer: fund-raising, public relations, connections with other
organizations. If so, clarifying this issue is a critical first step.

Recommendations for action

For case #1 (in the preceding list), when no input is desired,
no advisory committee should be established. If administrators
are interested in some support or service activities from an
advisory committee, then they should make it clear in the invitation to members and in the charge to the committee. They
should call it other than an "advisory committee"—one that
more closely represents what they are looking for, perhaps
"volunteer support network." The clearer the definition of
the committee's scope and function for prospective members,

the better. With clear communication, administrators can avoid a common problem of advisory committees—disgruntled members who think they were asked to give advice when what administrators really wanted was their service.

Case #2 calls for a paper or ceremonial advisory committee. If administrators clearly do not want input, a committee should be set up to meet once or twice a year. The meeting should be largely social, with perhaps some presentations by faculty or staff about some new programs. Again, it is best to make clear the ceremonial nature of such a committee when inviting members. Prospective members should be told what the expectations are for advice and for support or service.

These first two cases require no real attention to group dynamics, just some clarity about goals and expectations and some honesty with potential members. Cases 3 through 6, however, are more complicated, requiring anything from the appearance of input to a truly independent advisory committee.

Case #3 should be avoided, as it seeks the *appearance* of input and is inherently dishonest and manipulative. Unfortunately, many institutional representatives have set up such advisory committees, consciously or not, especially when the advisory committee is mandated and the staff or director does not want it. Instead, they give lip service to advisory input, contributing to committee members' disillusionment and disappointment, by limiting membership to those within the organization if they can get away with it and by using outsiders only if they have some programmatic ties or loyalty. They maintain the right to select and socialize new members. If the external mandate requires frequent meetings, the meetings are held, but staff are always present and always set the agenda. When they can, they limit the group's formal decision making, and, when possible, they chair the meetings themselves. If required to, they appoint a chair from outside the institution but try to keep it as nominal a role as possible, ideally limited to *just* chairing the meetings. They keep their mandate to the committee as vague as possible and limit access to information about the program as much as possible.

Case #4 is the first scenario in which administrators actually want some advice, although they choose to limit it to peripheral issues or to the committee's working as a sounding board for new ideas. The group is built with more outsiders, selected with care to include people knowledgeable enough to provide useful feedback. It is best to be clear with the committee about the scope of its advisory input. It is possible to have more regular meetings, even an outside chair, so long as members are selected and socialized to understand that their advisory role will be limited. Committee members need real information about the program so they can give useful input, although their access should be controlled so it can be carefully focused on the desired issues. Administrators should be honest about the committee's limited input, clearly outlining it in the written mandate to the committee.

Administrators should be honest about the committee's limited input.

Case #5, seeking substantive input on critical matters, requires a diverse and independent membership. The committee should be encouraged to exhibit a certain amount of independence by allowing real leadership to be exercised by an outside chair. Administrators might also consider a joint process for selecting and socializing new members. Administrators should retain the ability to set the agenda, probably restricting somewhat access to information to go along with that agenda.

For case #6, a truly independent advisory committee, administrators give to the committee control of the agenda and total access to information. To ensure that this independence cannot be easily tampered with, the committee should have the authority to select and socialize new members, have a clear mandate to make decisions as a body, and receive formal responses to formal suggestions.

Practical Advice for Committee Members
A similar exercise makes sense for prospective advisory committee members. The biggest source of tension and disgruntled committee members is the mismatch between members' expectations and the realities of the committee's work, but they can be minimized if individuals, before agreeing to join a committee, clarify their own goals and do some research on the committee.

Clarifying goals
The first step for prospective advisory committee members is to clarify their own goals. What is it that makes serving on the committee appealing? Is the chief commitment to the institution, to the students, or to a vision of what the program's or institution's work should be? Do the social aspects

of working with other volunteers matter? Is the most important motivation to do some good? Is it to learn something or to share expertise? Is it to advance a career or develop a connection or skill that can lead to a change in a career? Is it important to work on an advisory committee that performs mostly service or support tasks, or should the committee advise the organization or program? How much time and effort will be involved in serving on the committee?

Seeking additional information

When asked to serve on an advisory committee, many people ask only how frequently the committee will meet or whether they have any obligations to raise funds. But the answers to some additional questions about key variables will affect the role of the committee. Who are the other members, and how were they selected and oriented? How long is the term, and how are advisers replaced? Are meetings largely social? Who chairs them and sets the agendas? What are the committee's functions? Prospective members should ask to see a handbook or guidelines, if they exist, and should determine what access they have to information about the program and what happens to the committee's suggestions. If the committee is ongoing, they should try to speak to some current committee members or to review minutes of past meetings.

Recommendations for action

With the information gathered, prospective members should make their best guess about the committee's focus. Is the committee oriented toward service and support, and is it important to them that it probably will not be called on to give advice? If having a chance to advise the administration is important, then where on the continuum from case #1 to case #6 does the advisory committee fall? If it is case #1 or case #2, how would it feel to be on a ceremonial committee or one that never meets, one whose only outcome is to add "committee membership" to one's resume. Is the director or staff genuinely interested in advice? Will the scope of the advice be broad or tightly circumscribed? Does that matter?

Going through this process of clarifying goals and gathering information before accepting an assignment on the committee should minimize a prospective member's chances for disappointment or disillusionment. A framework exists for reflecting on goals—the individual's, the institution's, and the committee's—and prospective members will know what they are getting into.

Implications of the Relativist View Of Advisory Committees

The relativist view of effective advisory committees discussed in this section could meet the perceived goals of the staff or administrators who work with advisory committees as well as those of individual committee members. Except for case #3, where staff try to create the *appearance* of advisory input, most of the scenarios providing insignificant amounts of advice are based on clear communication and relatively high degrees of honesty. The truth-in-packaging approach of case #1 and case #2 should probably lead to more satisfactory experiences with advisory committees for everyone. If members know what they are getting into, they are less likely to be disillusioned about their roles. Paper or ceremonial committees are thus what the institutional representatives and the members want. Participation on a committee that provides a high level of service but little advice can similarly be negotiated in advance, minimizing the disappointments.

This self-selection and honesty can reduce dissatisfaction and conflict for committee members and staff, but what are the costs of this relativistic approach for the larger society? For example, external funders sometimes require advisory committees to ensure accountability, relevant programs, and responsiveness to different populations. Most funders lack the capacity for any significant monitoring, however, so what really happens in advisory committees is negotiated between institutional representatives and committee members themselves. If everyone is happy with a paper committee, it might satisfy them, but the goals of the external mandate are not being met.

On a broader level, if advisory committees are seen as important mechanisms to help institutions of higher education adapt to and respond to society, something is lost if the opportunity to receive advice is negotiated away by the mutual consent of staff and committee members. For instance, it makes sense from the perspective of the larger society that an organization have an advisory board with representation from a diverse mix of genders, ethnic groups, and races. But what if the committee meets only once a year for a ceremonial dinner? If the staff and committee members have followed truth-in-packaging guidelines, they could all be quite satisfied. But, in the broadest sense, society is the loser by failing to have in place a mechanism that can help these organizations respond to the needs of all members of society. What can external funders and others do to encourage the genuine use of advisory input?

The two following suggestions take two different tacks. One assumes that many institutional representatives will continue to be uninterested in advisory input and proposes ways to encourage the development of more independent advisory committees as a way to pressure them. The second looks at how the decision-making culture within an organization can be changed to make deans, directors, and staff more open to external advice.

Mandate conditions to foster independent committees

Funders, accreditors, and others in positions to mandate advisory committees can, just like institutional representatives and committee members, use the committee's membership, meetings, and mandate to try to get the type of advisory group they want (see table 6 on p. 54). Although they cannot create activist, independent advisory groups, they can mandate the conditions that would make it more likely for them to develop, promoting the development of a cohesive group spirit that might be strong enough to provide input even when staff and administrators do not want it. Because compliance with some existing regulations is so poor, external funders might do well to add a fourth "M"—monitoring—to ensure that membership is constructed and committees operated as prescribed.

Change the context for decision making within organizations

A second approach focuses on the way organizations incorporate advice into their decision making. The attitude of deans, directors, faculty, and staff toward input from an advisory committee is the single most important determinant of whether a committee's advice will be used. As long as the attitude toward improvement in most organizations is characterized by comments like "If it ain't broke, don't fix it," suggestions from advisory groups will be just one more complication, one more piece of input trying to influence organizational decision making. As long as administrators, faculty, and staff believe that the answers to the problems of their programs and institutions lie *within* their organizations, advisory committees will remain window dressing.

Input from advisory committees will be more widely used only when organizations develop a fundamentally different context for decision making. Two ideas from the business sector might help create these different contexts. *Strategic planning*, with its emphasis on using an "open systems approach to steering an enterprise over time through uncertain environmental waters" (Cope 1987, p. 3), gives considerably more weight in decision making to the external inputs that advisory committees can provide. Strategic planning overturns the common assumption that solutions to problems are internal and seeks to position the organization to take advantage of its position in the external environment. Advisory committees can be key vehicles for this reorientation.

Similarly, the movement toward *total quality management* replaces complacency with the notion of continuous improvement (Chaffee and Sherr 1992, p. 5). By emphasizing more information about the organization's processes and the satisfaction of the customers or clients, TQM can create the conditions for a higher value to be placed on advisory input, especially from people who are seen as stakeholders or clients of the institution.

Strategic planning and total quality management help change organizational culture so administrators and staff who work with advisory committees can develop different attitudes toward their input. But these major changes in institutional culture are difficult to bring about. Greater use of advisory committees requires the institutional culture to support managers, not just in developing the skills to run an advisory committee, but also in gaining skills for dealing with the diverse input and complexities greater use might bring. Changes like strategic planning and TQM move toward more open participation in management and will support the changes that will make it easier for advisory committees to serve as mechanisms for institutional and programmatic improvement.

REFERENCES

The Educational Resources Information Center (ERIC) Clearinghouse on Higher Education abstracts and indexes the current literature on higher education for inclusion in ERIC's data base and announcement in ERIC's monthly bibliographic journal, *Resources in Education* (RIE). Most of these publications are available through the ERIC Document Reproduction Service (EDRS). For publications cited in this bibliography that are available from EDRS, ordering number and price code are included. Readers who wish to order a publication should write to the ERIC Document Reproduction Service, 7420 Fullerton Rd., Suite 110, Springfield, VA 22153-2852. (Phone orders with VISA or MasterCard are taken at 800-443-ERIC or 703-440-1400.) When ordering, please specify the document (ED) number. Documents are available as noted in microfiche (MF) and paper copy (PC). If you have the price code ready when you call EDRS, an exact price can be quoted. The last page of the latest issue of *Resources in Education* also has the current cost, listed by code.

Alberger, Patricia L., ed. 1981. *How to Work Effectively with Alumni Boards.* Washington, D.C.: Council for the Advancement and Support of Education. ED 214 434. 86 pp. MF–01; PC not available EDRS.

American Association of State Colleges and Universities. 1989. "Key Success Factors for an Undergraduate Computer Information Systems Program." Model Programs Inventory Project. ED 306 876. 15 pp. MF–01; PC–01.

Anderson, John C., and Larry Moore. 1978. "The Motivation to Volunteer." *Journal of Voluntary Action Research* 7(4): 120–29.

Arbuckle, Margaret, and Lynn Murray. 1989. *Building Systems for Professional Growth: An Action Guide.* Andover, Mass.: Regional Labs for Educational Improvement of the Northeast and the Islands.

Axelrod, Nancy. 1991. *Creating and Renewing Advisory Boards: Strategies for Success.* Washington, D.C.: National Center for Nonprofit Boards.

Baker, Ronald E., and Bruce A. Ostertag. 1981. "Community College Handicapped Student Programs and Advisory Committees." ED 212 339. 16 pp. MF–01; PC–01.

Biagi, Bob. 1978. *Working Together: A Manual for Helping Groups Work More Effectively.* Citizen Involvement Training Project. Amherst: Univ. of Massachusetts.

Blake, Brian, Billy Beach, and Oscar Hopkins. 1976. "Helping Committee Members Become More Active." *Journal of Extension* 14(1): 16–22.

Bok, Derek. 1982. *Beyond the Ivory Tower.* Cambridge, Mass.: Harvard Univ. Press.

Borden, Jill. 1984. *Volunteerism in Adult Education: A Guidebook for Increasing the Scope and Quality of Volunteer Programs in Adult Education.* Phoenix, Ariz.: Phoenix Union High School District. ED 253 644. 218 pp. MF–01; PC–09.

Brawer, Florence B., and Allen Gates. 1981. "Advisory Committees
to the Humanities: A Handbook." Topical Paper No. 74. Los
Angeles: ERIC Clearinghouse for Junior Colleges. ED 210 066. 29
pp. MF–01; PC–02.

Brockman, R. John. 1982. "Advisory Boards in Technical Communications Programs and Classes." *Technical Writing Teacher* 9(3):
137–46.

Bromert, Jane Doyle. 1984. "College Search Committees." *ERIC Di-
gest* 84-2. Washington, D.C.: American Association of University
Administrators. ED 284 511. 5 pp. MF–01; PC–01.

Brudney, Jeffrey. 1990. *Fostering Volunteer Programs in the Public
Sector: Planning, Initiating, and Managing Voluntary Activities.*
San Francisco: Jossey-Bass.

Cadwalader, D., and R. Daugherty. 1989. "Effectiveness of Needs
Assessment and Advisory Committees in Planning and Implemen-
tation of Voluntarism In-Service Education." In *Developing Human
Capital through Extension Leadership Programs,* edited by Eliza-
beth B. Bolton and Lynn White. Proceedings of the Leadership
Development Seminar, August 6, Manhattan, Kansas. Gainesville:
Univ. of Florida. ED 316 355. 251 pp. MF–01; PC–11.

California State Dept. of Education. 1988. *Community Advisory Committee Guidelines.* 2d ed. Sacramento: Author. ED 305 808. 78 pp.
MF–01; PC not available EDRS.

Callaghan, Marty. 1986. "Gearing Up with Good Advice." *Currents*
12(5): 34–40.

Caparosa, Carol. October 1984. "Building Better Boards." *Community
and Junior College Journal* 55: 42–46.

Carroll, Richard. 1981. *Advanced Concepts in Structuring and Util-
izing Local Advisory Councils and Craft Committees.* Harrisburg:
Pennsylvania State Advisory Council for Vocational Education. ED
209 479. 42 pp. MF–01; PC–02.

Chaffee, E., and L. Sherr. 1992. *Quality: Transforming Postsecondary
Education.* ASHE-ERIC Higher Education Report No. 3. Washington, D.C.: Association for the Study of Higher Education. ED 351
922. 145 pp. MF–01; PC–06.

Childress, Ronald B. 1984. "A State-Level Model for Collaboration
among Teacher Education Institutions." ED 276 687. 15 pp. MF–
01; PC–01.

Cochran, Leslie, Allen Phelps, and Linda Cochran. 1980. *Advisory
Committees in Action: An Educational/Occupational/Community
Partnership.* Boston: Allyn & Bacon.

Cohen, Allan, Stephen Fink, Herman Gadon, and Robin Willits. 1988.
Effective Behavior in Organizations. Homewood, Ill.: Irwin.

Cope, Robert. 1987. *Opportunity from Strength: Strategic Planning
Clarified with Case Examples.* ASHE-ERIC Higher Education Report
No. 8. Washington, D.C.: Association for the Study of Higher Edu-

cation. ED 296 694. 149 pp. MF–01; PC–06.

Corley, Sherie P. 1988. "The Advisory Committee and Its Role in Program Planning at the Community College." ED 297 793. 23 pp. MF–01; PC–01.

Cuninggim, Merrimon. 1985. "The Pros and Cons of Advisory Committees." Washington, D.C.: Association of Governing Boards of Universities and Colleges. ED 263 811. 23 pp. MF–01; PC–01.

Dahl, Bonnie. 1986. "A Principal's Perspective: Lessons Learned from a Partnership Experience." Paper presented at an annual meeting of the American Educational Research Association, April 16–20, San Francisco, California. ED 274 091. 6 pp. MF–01; PC–01.

Davidson, George, et al. 1991. "The Governance of a Collaborative Teacher Education Program: The Emergence of New Structures and New Roles." ED 338 583. 9 pp. MF–01; PC–01.

Dearmin, Evalyn T. 1982. *University Teacher Education Councils.* Chicago: John Howard Association. ED 292 753. 48 pp. MF–01; PC–02.

Doti, James. 1989. "Business Advisory Councils Mini-Workshop." Paper presented at the AACSB fall 1989/winter 1990 seminars and workshops, November 8, Chicago, Illinois.

Dyer, Delwyn A., and Oscar M. Williams. 1991. *Developing Effective Boards, Councils, and Commissions.* Rev. ed. Blacksburg: Virginia Polytechnic Institute and State Univ., Center for Volunteer Development. ED 340 913. 28 pp. MF–01; PC–02.

Educational Development Center. 1987. *Vocational-Technical Advisory Committees: A Guide to Effective Utilization.* Quincy, Mass.: Dept. of Education.

Ellis, S. 1986. *From the Top Down: The Executive Role in Volunteer Program Success.* Philadelphia: Energize Association.

Emporia State University 1985. *Connections: A Model for Collaborative Preservice Teacher Education.* Emporia, Kans.: Author. ED 267 047. 47 pp. MF–01; PC–02.

Falk, David S., and Gerald Ray Miller. 1993. "How Do You Cut $45 Million from Your Institution's Budget?" *Educational Record* 74(4): 32–38.

Finch, Curtis, and Robert McGough. 1982. *Administering and Supervising Occupational Education.* Englewood Cliffs, N.J.: Prentice-Hall.

Garrity, Raymond J. 1984. "The Role of the Advisory Committee: Curricular Excellence." *Community and Junior College Journal* 55(2): 40–41.

Gibson, Molly. 1986. "The Volunteer View." *CASE Currents* 12(4): 64.

Gleberzon, William. 1981. "Seniors in Action: A Case Study of Participation at the University of Toronto by the Senior Alumni Association." Toronto: Univ. of Toronto, Dept. of Alumni Affairs. ED 216 594. 14 pp. MF–01; PC–01.

Goodale, Celia. 1981. "What the Volunteer Expects of the Staff." In

How to Work Effectively with Alumni Boards, edited by Patricia
L. Alberger. Washington, D.C.: Council for the Advancement and
Support of Education. ED 214 434. 86 pp. MF–01; PC not available
EDRS.

Gratz, Robert, and Philip Salem. 1989. "Communication across the
Boundary." In *Maximizing Opportunities through External Relations,* edited by Daniel Seymour. New Directions for Higher Education No. 68. San Francisco: Jossey-Bass.

Green, Susan K., et al. 1984. "Volunteer Motivation and Its Relationship to Satisfaction and Future Volunteering." ED 251 640. 15 pp.
MF–01; PC–01.

Gross, Raymond. 1980. "A Guide for Developing the Hahnemann
School of Respiratory Therapy Advisory Committee." Doctoral prac-
ticum, Nova Univ. ED 200 161. 32 pp. MF–01; PC–02.

Hackman, J.R., and R.E. Walton. 1986. "Leading Groups in Organizations." In *Designing Effective Work Groups,* edited by Paul
Goodman. San Francisco: Jossey-Bass.

Hannah, Michael T., and John H. Freeman. 1978. "The Population
Ecology of Organizations." In *Environments and Organizations,*
edited by Marshall W. Meyer. San Francisco: Jossey-Bass.

Hartley, Maurice. 1980. "Cooperative Education Advisory Councils:
Characteristics and Contributions." *Journal of Cooperative Education* 17(1): 16–25.

Hawkins, Layton, Charles Prosser, and John C. Wright. 1951. *Development of Vocational Education.* Chicago: American Technical
Society.

Henderson, Karla. 1981. "Motivating the 4-H Volunteer." *Journal of
Extension* 19(1): 19–27.

Hickey, Delina R., and David B. Andrews. 1993. "Creating Successful
Partnerships." *Educational Record* 74(3): 40–45.

Houle, Cyril O. 1990. *Governing Boards: Their Nature and Nurture.*
San Francisco: Jossey-Bass.

Ibrahim, Hilmi, et al. 1987. *Effective Parks and Recreation Boards
and Commissions.* Reston, Va.: American Alliance for Health, Phys-
ical Education, Recreation, and Dance. ED 290 713. 231 pp. MF–
01; PC not available EDRS.

Ilsley, Paul J. 1990. *Enhancing the Volunteer Experience: New Insights
on Strengthening Volunteer Participation, Learning, and Commitment.* San Francisco: Jossey-Bass.

Independent Sector. 1987. "The Constitution and the Independent
Sector. Working Papers." Proceedings of the Spring Research
Forum, March 19–20, New York, New York. Washington, D.C.:
Author. ED 302 111. 511 pp. MF–02; PC–21.

Johnson, D., and F. Johnson. 1975. *Joining Together: Group Theory
and Skills.* Englewood Cliffs, N.J.: Prentice-Hall.

Johnson, Janet Rogers-Clarke. 1982. "Perceptions of Factors Affecting
the Relative Effectiveness of Temporary Blue Ribbon State Com-

missions." Ph.D. dissertation, Univ. of Denver. ED 222 160. 220 pp. MF–01; PC–09.

Katz, Daniel, and Robert Kahn. 1966. *The Social Psychology of Organizations.* New York: John Wiley & Sons.

Keller, George. 1983. *Academic Strategy: The Management Revolution in American Higher Education.* Baltimore: Johns Hopkins Univ. Press.

Keller, J.M. 1983. "Motivational Design of Instruction." In *Instructional Design Theories and Models: An Overview of Their Current Status,* edited by C. Reiguluth. Hillsdale, N.J.: Lawrence Erlbaum Associates.

Kempton, Rodney. 1980. "Concepts in Volunteer Management." *Journal of Extension* 18(5): 19–23.

Kimberly, John R. 1981. "Initiation, Innovation, and Institutionalization in the Creation Process." In *The Organizational Life Cycle: Issues in the Creation, Transformation, and Decline of Organizations,* edited by John R. Kimberly and Robert H. Miles. San Francisco: Jossey-Bass.

King, Sam W. 1960. *Organization and the Effective Use of Advisory Committees.* Washington D.C.: U.S. Government Printing Office.

Knowledge Network for All Americans. 1992. *Winning the War against Ignorance: Empowering Public Schools.* Arlington, Va.: Author. ED 351 771. 86 pp. MF–01; PC–04.

Lacoursier, R. 1980. *The Life Cycle of Groups.* New York: Human Science Press.

Laney, James. 1984. "Using Visiting Committees." *AGB Reports* 26(3): 31–33.

Larson, Wendy. 1990. "For Adults Only: How Three Colleges Deliver Their Messages to Nontraditional Recruits." *Currents* 16(6): 38–40.

Lawrence, P.R., and J.W. Lorsch. 1967. *Organization and Environment.* Boston: Harvard Univ., Graduate School of Business Administration.

Light, John. 1982. *A Practitioner's Guide to Using and Meeting with Advisory Groups.* Columbus: National Center for Research in Vocational Education. ED 237 120. 68 pp. MF–01; PC–03.

Lillestol, Jane M. 1992. "Blue Chip Board." *Currents* 18(2): 23–26.

McClelland, D.C. 1976. *The Achievement Motivation.* 2d ed. New York: Irvington.

Maryland State Advisory Council on Vocational-Technical Education. 1984. "Vocational-Technical Education: Guidelines for Local Advisory Councils." Baltimore: Author. ED 256 895. 22 pp. MF–01; PC–01.

Maslow, A.H. 1970. *Motivation and Personality.* 2d ed. New York: Harper & Row.

Massachusetts Dept. of Education. 1985. *1985 Vocational Advisory Committee Survey of Chapter 74 Approved Vocational Programs.* Quincy: Author.

———. 1986. *1986 Vocational Advisory Committee Survey of Chapter*

74 *Approved Vocational Programs.* Quincy: Author.

Mayer, Lynne S. 1981. *Advisory Committees within Marshall University, 1981–82.* Huntington, W.Va.: Marshall Univ. ED 212 249. 57 pp. MF–01; PC–03.

Meyer, Marshall W. 1978. "Introduction: Recent Developments in Organizational Research and Theory." In *Environments and Organizations,* edited by Marshall W. Meyer. San Francisco: Jossey-Bass.

Miles, R.H. 1980. *Macro-Organizational Behavior.* Glenview Ill.: Scott, Foresman.

Miles, Robert H., and W. Alan Randolph. 1981. "Influence of Organizational Learning Styles on Early Development." In *The Organizational Life Cycle: Issues in the Creation, Transformation, and Decline of Organizations,* edited by John R. Kimberly and Robert H. Miles. San Francisco: Jossey-Bass.

Miller, Robert W. 1987. "Using Evaluation to Support the Program Advisory Function: A Case Study of Evaluator–Program Advisory Committee Collaboration." *Evaluation and Program Planning* 10: 281–88.

Murk, Peter J., and Jane F. Stephan. 1990. "Volunteers Enhance the Quality of Life in a Community—Or How to Get Them, Train Them, and Keep Them." ED 326 639. 14 pp. MF–01; PC–01.

National Advisory Committee on Black Higher Education and Black Colleges and Universities. 1982. *Higher Education Equity: The Crisis of Appearance versus Reality Revisited.* Final report. Washington, D.C.: Author. ED 255 122. 178 pp. MF–01; PC–08.

Nebraska State Advisory Council for Vocational Education. 1982. *Handbook for Local Vocational Education Advisory Councils: The People Speak.* Lincoln: Author. ED 235 303. 28 pp. MF–01; PC–02.

New York Governor's Advisory Committee for Black Affairs. 1988. "Status Needs Positive Change." Report of the Subcommittee on the Immigrant Community of African Descent. ED 348 412. 166 pp. MF–01; PC–07.

O'Connell, Brian. 1985. *The Board Member's Book.* New York: Foundation Center.

Oen, Urban T. 1985. "Establishing and Conducting Meetings of a General and Specialized Occupation Advisory Committee." ED 261 156. 38 pp. MF–01; PC–02.

Office of the State Director for Vocational Education. 1987. *Guidelines for the Development, Implementation, and Operation of School Vocational Education Councils.* Honolulu: Author. ED 297 793. 34 pp. MF–01; PC not available EDRS.

Ohio State University. 1985. *Maintain[ing] an Occupational Advisory Committee.* 2d ed. Professional Teacher Education Module Series. Columbus: Ohio State Univ., National Center for Research in Vocational Education. ED 255 669. 38 pp. MF–01; PC–02.

Oklahoma State Council for Vocational Education. 1988. *Handbook for Instructors and Advisory Committee Members.* Oklahoma City: Author. ED 311 214. 29 pp. MF–01; PC–02.

Oswald, Moody. 1984. "Revitalizing an Old Medium: Using Advisory Committees." In *Collaboration: Vocational Education and the Private Sector.* Arlington, Va.: American Vocational Association.

Parry-Hill, Joseph W., Jr. 1981. "Highlights from Two Recent Studies on the Use of Citizen Advisory Groups in the North Carolina Community Colleges." Raleigh: North Carolina State Advisory Council on Education. ED 210 054. 9 pp. MF–01; PC–01.

Pearce, Jone. 1980. "Apathy or Self-Interest: The Volunteer's Avoidance of Leadership Roles." *Journal of Voluntary Action Research* 9(1): 85–94.

Pennings, Johannes. 1981. "Environmental Influences on the Creation Process." In *The Organizational Life Cycle: Issues in the Creation, Transformation, and Decline of Organizations,* edited by John R. Kimberly and Robert H. Miles. San Francisco: Jossey-Bass.

Pfeffer, J., and G.R. Salancik. 1978. *The External Control of Organizations.* New York: Harper & Row.

Popovics, Alexander, and P. Jonas. 1992. "A Comprehensive Participative Planning Model for Small Liberal Arts Colleges." Paper presented at an annual forum of the Association for Institutional Research, May 10–13, Atlanta, Georgia. ED 349 875. 20 pp. MF–01; PC–01.

Reynolds, Florence. 1979. "Getting Professional Support for Programs with Problems." *Community College Journalist* 8(1): 21–22.

Rice, Eric, and Douglas A. Buescher. 1984. *Vocational Instructional Program Advisory Committee Resource Guide.* Washington, D.C.: International Management and Development Institute, Office of Vocational and Adult Education. ED 250 459. 190 pp. MF–01; PC–08.

Riendeau, Albert. 1977. *Advisory Committees for Occupational Education: A Guide to Organization and Operation.* New York: McGraw-Hill.

Rowland, A.W. 1980. "Cultivating Community Support." In *Effective Community Relations,* edited by Howard Howland. New Directions for Institutional Advancement No 10. San Francisco: Jossey-Bass.

Ryan, Patricia M. 1993. "A Collaborative Restructuring Teacher Education Program: A Teachers Teaching Teachers Institute." Paper presented at the 73rd Annual Meeting of the Association of Teacher Educators, February 13–17, Los Angeles, California. ED 355 229. 7 pp. MF–01; PC 01.

Salsini, Barbara. 1986. "Let an Advisory Committee Share Management Problems." *College Store Journal* 53(5): 33–34.

Schein, Edgar. 1969. *Process Consultation: Its Role in Organizational Development.* Reading, Mass.: Addison Wesley.

Schindler-Rainman, Eva, and R. Lippitt. 1975. *The Volunteer Community: Creative Use of Human Resources.* San Diego: University Associates.

Schug, Mark. 1982. "Improving Teacher Education by Using Program Advisory Committees." *Social Studies Teacher* 73: 148–50.

Scott, Robert A. 1988. "An Advisory Council for Strategic Planning." *AGB Reports* 30(3): 12–13.

Seymour, Daniel T. 1989. *Maximizing Opportunities through External Relations*. New Directions for Higher Education No. 68. San Francisco: Jossey-Bass.

Silver, Gerald. 1988. "Using Advisory Boards in Academic Administration." Paper presented at an annual meeting of the American Association for Adult and Continuing Education, October 31–November 5. ED 305 881. 12 pp. MF–01; PC–01.

———. 1992. "Advisory Boards: Academic Partnerships That Work." ED 343 626. 10 pp. MF–01; PC–01.

Smith, D.H. 1981. "Altruism, Volunteers, and Volunteering." *Journal of Voluntary Action Research* 10(1): 21–36.

Sweningson, Sally. 1984. *Connecting: A Guidebook for Community Education Council Effectiveness*. St. Paul: College of St. Thomas, Community Education Center. ED 287 000. 29 pp. MF–01; PC not available EDRS.

Teitel, Lee. 1991. "The Transformation of a Community College." *Community College Review* 19(1): 7–13.

Thiers, Naomi. 1992. "Speaking Volumes: A Comprehensive Handbook Can Keep Your Alumni Board on Target and on Schedule." *Currents* 18(2): 28.

Thompson, Hugh. 1984. "Are Boards Other than Trustees Needed?" *AGB Reports* 26(3): 27–30.

"Toward a Trouble-free Board." 1992. *Currents* 18(2): 33–36.

Valencia Community College. 1980. "The Black Advisory Committee of Valencia Community College. Guidelines." Orlando: Author. ED 229 059. 11 pp. MF–01; PC–01.

Van Dersal, William R. 1974. *The Successful Supervisor in Government and Business*. New York: Harper & Row.

Van Til, J. 1988. *Mapping the Third Sector: Voluntarism in a Changing Social Economy*. New York: Foundation Center.

Virginia Highlands Community College. 1993. *Citizens Advisory Committees for Virginia Highlands Community College: A Book of Information, Policies, and Procedures*. Rev. ed. Abingdon, Va.: Author. ED 363 370. 46 pp. MF–01; PC–02.

Walters, Norma J. 1986. *The State Advisory Council on Vocational Education*. Auburn Univ., Center for Vocational and Adult Education. ED 267 300. 29 pp. MF–01; PC–02.

Welch, Robert. 1989. "Administering Programs for Special Populations." *Equity and Excellence* 24(3): 72–73.

Wilson, Douglas. 1981. "How to Educate and Motivate Your Alumni Board." In *How to Work Effectively with Alumni Boards*, edited by Patricia L. Alberger. Washington, D.C.: Council for the Advancement and Support of Education. ED 214 434. 86 pp. MF–01; PC not available EDRS.

Winsor, Jerry, et al. 1992. "Establishing Professional Advisory Councils for Communications Programs." Warrensburg: Central Missouri State Univ. ED 352 692. 17 pp. MF–01; PC–01.

INDEX

A
action, recommendations for, 82-83
ad hoc advisory groups, definition of, 4
advice
        avoidance of, 30-32
        presentation of, 45
        what wanted by administrators, 79
Advisory Committee, definition of, iii, 3-5
        link into the external community, 5
        meets regularly on a long-term basis, 4
        volunteer nature of, 3
African American enrollment, at Valencia Community College, 7, 14
African descent, committee on needs of immigrants of, 6
AGB Reports, 65
altruism, seldom only reason for volunteering, 33

B
Black Higher Education and Black Colleges and Universities, 6
blue ribbon commissions, definition of, 4
boundary
        activities, support of, 11-12
        personnel, roles of, 11

C
California
        community colleges, handicaps adaptations committees, 7
        Department of Education guidelines for committees, 52
categories of work, 5
calling a meeting, power to do so, 64
campus wide advisory committees, 7
Carl Perkins Act of 1984, 19
Central Missouri State University,
        keeping programs up to date, 8
        legitimacy, gaining, 14
commitment
        of committee members, 63
        types of, 22-34, 40
Committee of Forty, 14
committee leadership, determination and duties of need
    definition, 46
committee powers, factors tending to
        decrease, 64
        increase, 63-64
community college, advisory committee jurisdictions, 8
conflict resolution, 45
coordinating mechanism, 17

New York committee on African descent immigrant needs, 6
non traditional programs, promoting legitimacy of, 14
norming
    process of, 52-53
    stage of group formation, 48

O

Ohio State University, advisory group as link to external
    community, 8
Oklahoma, home economics sessions assessment, 13
opposition, use of committees to defuse, 15
organizational factors influencing committee development, 54
orienting committee members, 69-70

P

participation of group members, 44
performance evaluation of group members, 45
performing stage in group formation, 47-49
Planning and establishing an Advisory Committee
    Appointment, 69
    Preliminary work, 65
    Selection, xv, 65-68. see also membership
    Size, 66
possibilities, matrix of, 40
pressures, committees as response to, 16
process, attention to required, 46

R

Ramapo College, corporate leaders advisory team, 7
recognition of advisory committee members, ways to, 74
recommendations for action, 79-81
relationships within an advisory committee, 43-44
relativist view of advisory committees, implications of, 83-84
Report, three divisions of this Higher Education, 1-2
role definition, need for in advisory committees, 25-26
rubber stamp committee, dissatisfaction from, 27-29

S

search committees, definition of, 4
secretary, role of in manipulating committee, 71-72
selection of Advisory Committee. see Planning and establishing
Seymour, Dan, xvii
Smith-Hughes Act of 1917, 19
storming stage of group formation, 48-49
staff attitude and expectations, 62-63
strategic planning, 85
structure, organizational development of, 71-72

successorship, control of, 64
support required, definition of by administrators necessary, 78-79

T

tasks of any group, 43
teacher preparation help, at University of Wisconsin, 8
third party input, advisory panel collects data, 13-14
Toronto, University advisory committee for gerontology
    program, 8
total quality management, 85

U

University of California at San Diego, 14-15
University of Richmond (Virginia), needs assessment, 13
University of Wisconsin at Milwaukee, teacher preparation
    help, 8

V

Valencia Community College, enrollment promote, 7, 14
visiting committees, definition of, 4
vocational advisory committees, themes with, 19
Vocational Education Act of 1963, 19

W

West Virginia, collaboration among teacher preparation
    institutions, 6
work plans, development and implementation is cyclical, 73

ASHE-ERIC HIGHER EDUCATION REPORTS

Since 1983, the Association for the Study of Higher Education (ASHE) and the Educational Resources Information Center (ERIC) Clearinghouse on Higher Education, a sponsored project of the School of Education and Human Development at The George Washington University, have cosponsored the *ASHE-ERIC Higher Education Report* series. The 1994 series is the twenty-third overall and the sixth to be published by the School of Education and Human Development at the George Washington University.

Each monograph is the definitive analysis of a tough higher education problem, based on thorough research of pertinent literature and institutional experiences. Topics are identified by a national survey. Noted practitioners and scholars are then commissioned to write the reports, with experts providing critical reviews of each manuscript before publication.

Eight monographs (10 before 1985) in the ASHE-ERIC Higher Education Report series are published each year and are available on individual and subscription bases. To order, use the order form on the last page of this book.

Qualified persons interested in writing a monograph for the ASHE-ERIC Higher Education Reports are invited to submit a proposal to the National Advisory Board. As the preeminent literature review and issue analysis series in higher education, we can guarantee wide dissemination and national exposure for accepted candidates. Execution of a monograph requires at least a minimal familiarity with the ERIC database, including *Resources in Education* and *Current Index to Jounals in Education.* The objective of these Reports is to bridge conventional wisdom with practical research. Prospective authors are strongly encouraged to call Dr. Fife at 800-773-3742.

For further information, write to
ASHE-ERIC Higher Education Reports
The George Washington University
1 Dupont Circle, Suite 630
Washington, DC 20036
Or phone (202) 296-2597, toll-free: 800-773-ERIC.
Write or call for a complete catalog.

ADVISORY BOARD

Barbara E. Brittingham
University of Rhode Island

Jay L. Chronister
University of Virginia

Rodolfo Z. Garcia
Michigan State University

Elizabeth M. Hawthorne
The Pennsylvania State University

Bruce Anthony Jones
University of Pittsburgh

L. Jackson Newell
University of Utah

Carolyn Thompson
State University of New York–Buffalo

CONSULTING EDITORS

Robert J. Barak
State Board of Regents, Iowa

J. Kent Caruthers
MGT of America, Inc.

Elsa Kircher Cole
The University of Michigan

Robert M. Hendrickson
The Pennsylvania State University

George D. Kuh
Indiana University–Bloomington

Barbara A. Lee
Rutgers University

Yvonna S. Lincoln
Texas A&M University

Frances Lucas-Tauchar
Emory University

Kathleen Manning
The University of Vermont

Laurence R. Marcus
New Jersey Department of Higher Education

Robert J. Menges
Northwestern University

Leila Moore
The Pennsylvania State University

Amaury Nora
University of Illinois–Chicago

Robert M. O'Neil
University of Virginia

C. Robert Pace
University of California–Los Angeles

Raymond V. Padilla
Arizona State University

Scott Rickard
Association of College Unions–International

G. Jeremiah Ryan
Harford Community College

Frances Stage
Indiana University–Bloomington

Kala Stroop
Southeast Missouri State University

Ellen Switkes
University of California–Oakland

Carolyn J. Thompson
State University of New York–Buffalo

Caroline Turner
University of Minnesota–Twin Cities

Sheila L. Weiner
Board of Overseers of Harvard College

Elizabeth A. Williams
University of Massachuetts–Amherst

Richard A. Yanikoski
De Paul University

REVIEW PANEL

Charles Adams
University of Massachusetts–Amherst

Louis Albert
American Association for Higher Education

Richard Alfred
University of Michigan

Philip G. Altbach
Boston College

Marilyn J. Amey
University of Kansas

Louis C. Attinasi, Jr.
University of Houston

Robert J. Barak
Iowa State Board of Regents

Alan Bayer
Virginia Polytechnic Institute and State University

John P. Bean
Indiana University

John M. Braxton
Vanderbilt University

Peter McE. Buchanan
Council for Advancement and
    Support of Education

John A. Centra
Syracuse University

Arthur W. Chickering
George Mason University

Shirley M. Clark
Oregon State System of Higher Education

Darrel A. Clowes
Virginia Polytechnic Institute and State University

John W. Creswell
University of Nebraska–Lincoln

Deborah DiCroce
Piedmont Virginia Community College

Richard Duran
University of California

Kenneth C. Green
University of Southern California

Edward R. Hines
Illinois State University

Marsha W. Krotseng
West Virginia State College and University Systems

George D. Kuh
Indiana University–Bloomington

Daniel T. Layzell
University of Wisconsin System

Meredith Ludwig
American Association of State Colleges and Universities

Mantha V. Mehallis
Florida Atlantic University

Robert J. Menges
Northwestern University

Toby Milton
Essex Community College

James R. Mingle
State Higher Education Executive Officers

Gary Rhoades
University of Arizona

G. Jeremiah Ryan
Harford Community College

Mary Ann Sagaria
Ohio State University

Daryl G. Smith
Claremont Graduate School

William Tierney
University of Southern California

Susan Twombly
University of Kansas

Harold Wechsler
University of Rochester

Michael J. Worth
The George Washington University

RECENT TITLES

1993 ASHE-ERIC Higher Education Reports

1. The Department Chair: New Roles, Responsibilities and Challenges
   Alan T. Seagren, John W. Creswell, and Daniel W. Wheeler

2. Sexual Harassment in Higher Education: From Conflict to Community
   Robert O. Riggs, Patricia H. Murrell, and JoAnn C. Cutting

3. Chicanos in Higher Education: Issues and Dilemmas for the 21st Century
   by Adalberto Aguirre, Jr., and Ruben O. Martinez

4. Academic Freedom in American Higher Education: Rights, Responsibilities, and Limitations
   by Robert K. Poch

5. Making Sense of the Dollars: The Costs and Uses of Faculty Compensation
   by Kathryn M. Moore and Marilyn J. Amey

6. Enhancing Promotion, Tenure and Beyond: Faculty Socialization as a Cultural Process
   by William G. Tierney and Robert A. Rhoads

7. New Perspectives for Student Affairs Professionals: Evolving Realities, Responsibilities and Roles
   by Peter H. Garland and Thomas W. Grace

8. Turning Teaching Into Learning: The Role of Student Responsibility in the Collegiate Experience
   by Todd M. Davis and Patricia Hillman Murrell

1992 ASHE-ERIC Higher Education Reports

1. The Leadership Compass: Values and Ethics in Higher Education
   John R. Wilcox and Susan L. Ebbs

2. Preparing for a Global Community: Achieving an International Perspective in Higher Education
   Sarah M. Pickert

3. Quality: Transforming Postsecondary Education
   Ellen Earle Chaffee and Lawrence A. Sherr

4. Faculty Job Satisfaction: Women and Minorities in Peril
   Martha Wingard Tack and Carol Logan Patitu

5. Reconciling Rights and Responsibilities of Colleges and Students: Offensive Speech, Assembly, Drug Testing, and Safety
   Annette Gibbs

6. Creating Distinctiveness: Lessons from Uncommon Colleges and Universities
   Barbara K. Townsend, L. Jackson Newell, and Michael D. Wiese

---

7. Instituting Enduring Innovations: Achieving Continuity of Change in Higher Education
   Barbara K. Curry

8. Crossing Pedagogical Oceans: International Teaching Assistants in U.S. Undergraduate Education
   Rosslyn M. Smith, Patricia Byrd, Gayle L. Nelson, Ralph Pat Barrett, and Janet C. Constantinides

1991 ASHE-ERIC Higher Education Reports

1. Active Learning: Creating Excitement in the Classroom
   Charles C. Bonwell and James A. Eison

2. Realizing Gender Equality in Higher Education: The Need to Integrate Work/Family Issues
   Nancy Hensel

3. Academic Advising for Student Success: A System of Shared Responsibility
   Susan H. Frost

4. Cooperative Learning: Increasing College Faculty Instructional Productivity
   David W. Johnson, Roger T. Johnson, and Karl A. Smith

5. High School–College Partnerships: Conceptual Models, Programs, and Issues
   Arthur Richard Greenberg

6. Meeting the Mandate: Renewing the College and Departmental Curriculum
   William Toombs and William Tierney

7. Faculty Collaboration: Enhancing the Quality of Scholarship and Teaching
   Ann E. Austin and Roger G. Baldwin

8. Strategies and Consequences: Managing the Costs in Higher Education
   John S. Waggaman

1990 ASHE-ERIC Higher Education Reports

1. The Campus Green: Fund Raising in Higher Education
   Barbara E. Brittingham and Thomas R. Pezzullo

2. The Emeritus Professor: Old Rank - New Meaning
   James E. Mauch, Jack W. Birch, and Jack Matthews

3. "High Risk" Students in Higher Education: Future Trends
   Dionne J. Jones and Betty Collier Watson

4. Budgeting for Higher Education at the State Level: Enigma, Paradox, and Ritual
   Daniel T. Layzell and Jan W. Lyddon

5. Proprietary Schools: Programs, Policies, and Prospects
   John B. Lee and Jamie P. Merisotis

6. College Choice: Understanding Student Enrollment Behavior
   Michael B. Paulsen

7. Pursuing Diversity: Recruiting College Minority Students
   Barbara Astone and Elsa Nuñez-Wormack

8. Social Consciousness and Career Awareness: Emerging Link
   in Higher Education
   John S. Swift, Jr.

1989 ASHE-ERIC Higher Education Reports

1. Making Sense of Administrative Leadership: The 'L' Word in
   Higher Education
   Estela M. Bensimon, Anna Neumann, and Robert Birnbaum

2. Affirmative Rhetoric, Negative Action: African-American and
   Hispanic Faculty at Predominantly White Universities
   Valora Washington and William Harvey

3. Postsecondary Developmental Programs: A Traditional Agenda
   with New Imperatives
   Louise M. Tomlinson

4. The Old College Try: Balancing Athletics and Academics in
   Higher Education
   John R. Thelin and Lawrence L. Wiseman

5. The Challenge of Diversity: Involvement or Alienation in the
   Academy?
   Daryl G. Smith

6. Student Goals for College and Courses: A Missing Link in Assessing and Improving Academic Achievement
   Joan S. Stark, Kathleen M. Shaw, and Malcolm A. Lowther

7. The Student as Commuter: Developing a Comprehensive Institutional Response
   Barbara Jacoby

8. Renewing Civic Capacity: Preparing College Students for Service
   and Citizenship
   Suzanne W. Morse

1988 ASHE-ERIC Higher Education Reports

1. The Invisible Tapestry: Culture in American Colleges and
   Universities
   George D. Kuh and Elizabeth J. Whitt

2. Critical Thinking: Theory, Research, Practice, and Possibilities
   Joanne Gainen Kurfiss

---

3. Developing Academic Programs: The Climate for Innovation
   Daniel T. Seymour

4. Peer Teaching: To Teach is To Learn Twice
   Neal A. Whitman

5. Higher Education and State Governments: Renewed Partnership, Cooperation, or Competition?
   Edward R. Hines

6. Entrepreneurship and Higher Education: Lessons for Colleges, Universities, and Industry
   James S. Fairweather

7. Planning for Microcomputers in Higher Education: Strategies for the Next Generation
   Reynolds Ferrante, John Hayman, Mary Susan Carlson, and Harry Phillips

8. The Challenge for Research in Higher Education: Harmonizing Excellence and Utility
   Alan W. Lindsay and Ruth T. Neumann

1987 ASHE-ERIC Higher Education Reports

1. Incentive Early Retirement Programs for Faculty: Innovative Responses to a Changing Environment
   Jay L. Chronister and Thomas R. Kepple, Jr.

2. Working Effectively with Trustees: Building Cooperative Campus Leadership
   Barbara E. Taylor

3. Formal Recognition of Employer-Sponsored Instruction: Conflict and Collegiality in Postsecondary Education
   Nancy S. Nash and Elizabeth M. Hawthorne

4. Learning Styles: Implications for Improving Educational Practices
   Charles S. Claxton and Patricia H. Murrell

5. Higher Education Leadership: Enhancing Skills through Professional Development Programs
   Sharon A. McDade

6. Higher Education and the Public Trust: Improving Stature in Colleges and Universities
   Richard L. Alfred and Julie Weissman

7. College Student Outcomes Assessment: A Talent Development Perspective
   Maryann Jacobi, Alexander Astin, and Frank Ayala, Jr.

8. Opportunity from Strength: Strategic Planning Clarified with Case Examples
   Robert G. Cope

ORDER FORM

Quantity   **Amount**

_____ Please begin my subscription to the 1994 *ASHE-ERIC*
Higher Education Reports at $98.00, 31% off the cover
price, starting with Report 1, 1994. Includes shipping. _____

_____ Please send a complete set of the 1993 *ASHE-ERIC*
Higher Education Reports at $98.00, 31% off the cover
price. Please add shipping charge, below.   _____

Individual reports are avilable at the following prices:
1993 and 1994, $18.00; 1988-1992, $17.00; 1980-1987, $15.00

SHIPPING CHARGES
For orders of more than 50 books, please call for shipping information.

Total Quantity:	1st three books	Ea. addl. book
U.S., 48 Contiguous States		
Ground:	$3.75	$0.15
2nd Day*:	8.25	1.10
Next Day*:	18.00	1.60
Alaska & Hawaii (2nd Day Only)*:	13.25	1.40

U.S. Territories and Foreign Countries: Please call for shipping information.
*Order will be shipping within 24 hours of request.
All prices shown on this form are subject to change.

PLEASE SEND ME THE FOLLOWING REPORTS:

Quantity	Report No.	Year	Title	Amount

Please check one of the following:

☐ Check enclosed, payable to GWU-ERIC.   **Subtotal:** _____

☐ Purchase order attached ($45.00 minimum).   **Shipping:** _____

☐ Charge my credit card indicated below: **Total Due:** _____

    ☐ Visa   ☐ MasterCard

Expiration Date _____

Name _____

Title _____

Institution _____

Address _____

City _____ State _____ Zip _____

Phone _____ Fax _____ Telex _____

Signature _____ Date _____

SEND ALL ORDERS TO: ASHE-ERIC Higher Education Reports
The George Washington University
One Dupont Cir., Ste. 630, Washington, DC 20036-1183
Phone: (202) 296-2597 • Toll-free: 800-773-ERIC